T0362914

PUBLISHED BY BOOM BOOKS

boombooks.biz

ABOUT THIS SERIES

....But after that, I realised that I knew very little about these parents of mine. They had been born about the start of the Twentieth Century, and they died in 1970 and 1980. For their last 20 years, I was old enough to speak with a bit of sense.

I could have talked to them a lot about their lives. I could have found out about the times they lived in.

But I did not. I know almost nothing about them really. Their courtship? Working in the pits? The Lock-out in the Depression? Losing their second child? Being dusted as a miner? The shootings at Rothbury? My uncles killed in the War? Love on the dole? There were hundreds, thousands of questions that I would now like to ask them. But, alas, I can't. It's too late.

Thus, prompted by my guilt, I resolved to write these books. They describe happenings that affected people, real people. The whole series is, to coin a modern phrase, designed to push your buttons, to make you remember and wonder at things forgotten.

The books might just let nostalgia see the light of day, so that oldies and youngies will talk about the past and re-discover a heritage otherwise forgotten. Hopefully, they will spark discussions between generations, and foster the asking and answering of questions that should not remain unanswered.

BORN IN 1947?

WHAT ELSE HAPPENED?

RON WILLIAMS

AUSTRALIAN SOCIAL HISTORY

BOOK 9 IN A SERIES OF 35
FROM 1939 to 1973

War Babies Years (1939 to 1945):   7 Titles

Baby Boom Years (1946 to 1960):   15 Titles

Post Boom Years (1961 to 1970):   13 Titles

BOOM, BOOM BABY, BOOM

BORN IN 1947?   WHAT ELSE HAPPENED?

Published by Boom Books, Wickham, NSW, Australia
Web: www.boombooks.biz
Email: email@boombooks.biz

Creator: Williams, Ron, 1934- author
Title: Born in 1947? : what else happened? / Ron Williams.
ISBN: 9780995354975 (paperback)
Australia--History--Miscellanea--20th century.

Cover images: National Archives of Australia.

A1200, L8923, Sir Isaac Isaacs;

A1200, L7774, bushwalkers with baby;

A1200, L46645, Don Bradman;

A1200, L4504, Reverend John Flynn;

A1200, L9554, shearing team at work.

CONTENTS

IMPORTANT PEOPLE AND EVENTS

Oz Prime Minister	Ben Chifley
Opposition Leader	Bob Menzies
Governor General	William McKell
Britain's Prime Minister	Clement Atlee
Britain's Opposition	Winston Churchill
US President	Harry Truman
British Monarch	King George VI
Heir to the Throne	Princess Elizabeth
Catholic Pope	Pope Pius XII

WINNER OF THE ASHES

1938	Drawn Series 1 - 1
1946 - 1947	Australia 3 - 0
1948	Australia 4 - 0

MELBOURNE CUP WINNERS

1946	Russia
1947	Hiraji
1948	Rimfire

ACADEMY AWARDS 1947

BEST ACTOR: Frederick March

BEST ACTRESS: Olivier de Havilland

BEST MOVIE: The Best Years of our Lives

PREFACE TO THE SERIES

This book is the 9th in a series of books that I have researched and written. It tells a story about a number of important or newsworthy Australia-centric events that happened in 1947. The series covers each of the years from 1939 to 1970 for a total of 32 books.

I developed my interest in writing these books a few years ago at a time when my children entered their teens. My own teens started in 1947, and I started trying to remember what had happened to me then. I thought of the big events first, like Saturday afternoon at the pictures, and cricket in the back yard, and the wonderful fun of going to Maitland on the train for school each day. Then I recalled some of the not-so-good things. I was an altar boy, and that meant three or four Masses a week. I might have thought I loved God at that stage, but I really hated his Masses. And the schoolboy bullies, like Greg Favell, and the hapless Freddie Bevan. Yet, to compensate for these, there was always the beautiful, black headed, blue-sailor-suited June Brown, who I was allowed to worship from a distance.

I also thought about my parents. Most of the major events that I lived through came to mind readily. But after that, I realised that I really knew very little about these parents of mine. They had been born about the start of the Twentieth Century, and they died in 1970 and 1980. For their last 20 years, I was old enough to speak with a bit of sense. I could have talked to them a lot about their lives. I could have found out about the times they lived in. But I did not. I know almost nothing about them really. Their courtship? Working in the pits? The Lock-out in the Depression?

Losing their second child? Being dusted as a miner? The shootings at Rothbury? My uncles killed in the war? There were hundreds, thousands of questions that I would now like to ask them. But, alas, I can't. It's too late.

Thus, prompted by my guilt, I resolved to write these books. They describe happenings that affected people, real people. In **1947,** there is some coverage of international affairs, but a lot more on social events within Australia. This book, and the whole series is, to coin a modern phrase, designed to push the reader's buttons, to make you remember and wonder at things forgotten. The books might just let nostalgia see the light of day, so that oldies and youngies will talk about the past and re-discover a heritage otherwise forgotten. Hopefully, they will spark discussions between generations, and foster the asking and the answering of questions that should not remain unanswered.

The sources of my material. I was born in 1934, so that I can remember well a great deal of what went on around me from 1939 onwards. But of course, the bulk of this book's material came from research. That meant that I spent many hours in front of a computer reading electronic versions of newspapers, magazines, Hansard, Ministers' Press releases and the like. My task was to sift out, **day-by-day**, those stories and events that would be of interest to the most readers. Then I supplemented these with materials from books, broadcasts, memoirs, biographies, government reports and statistics. And I talked to old-timers, one-on-one, and in organised groups, and to Baby Boomers about their recollections. People with stories to tell come out of the woodwork, and talk no end about the tragic and funny and commonplace events that have shaped their lives.

The presentation of each book. For each year, the end result is a collection of Chapters on many of the topics that concerned ordinary people in that year. I think I have covered most of the major issues that people then were interested in. On the other hand, in some cases I have dwelt a little on minor frivolous matters, perhaps to the detriment of more sober considerations. Still, in the long run, this makes the book more readable, and hopefully it will convey adequately the spirit of the times.

I have been **deliberately national in outlook**, so that readers elsewhere will feel comfortable that I am talking about matters that affected them personally. After all, housing shortages and strikes and juvenile delinquency involved **all** Australians, and other issues, such as problems overseas, had no State component in them. Overall, I expect I can make you wonder, remember, rage and giggle equally, no matter where you hail from.

INTRO TO 1947

Australia in 1947 was a lucky country. That fact might not have been so obvious to the ordinary householder struggling with all the post-war problems that I will soon describe. **But it was still true.** In England, and in Europe, and China and Japan, and a dozen other parts of the world, citizens of county after country had been bombed, or invaded, starved, imprisoned, tortured, or killed. Entire families had been wiped out, large and small cities destroyed, all infrastructure was unusable, and crops and food supplies were totally inadequate.

We in Australia had seen some of this. In particular, we had seen our beautiful silly young men shipped off to foreign climes to be pointlessly killed and maimed by the beautiful silly young men from other countries. We had seen our crops and farms and infrastructure run down, our households disrupted by **war-time conscription** for all sorts of jobs, our food rationed, and the dreams of millions of young and old people shattered.

But **we had got off lightly**, compared to other places. We got off lightly **during the war**, and also **now that it was over**. Right now **in Europe** there were tens of millions of good, sensible, formerly-happy families, trudging slowly from east to west, or west to east, looking for a place they could call home. Their houses had been destroyed, their menfolk often killed or maimed, their lives were shattered. They had almost no food, only rags to stand up in. They shuffled along in vast columns of refugees, day after day. They stopped only to bury their dead, by the road, and they headed for places that they knew would be just as bad as the ones they had left.

In Britain, the situation was a little better. The main problems there were the shortage of accommodation, and the shortage of food and other products that were lumped together under the governmental term of "austerity." What was **implied** here was that while food, and clothing and all sorts of goods were hard to get, this was **only for a short time**, and was not even a shortage. No, was the official theme, we have won the war, so we no longer have shortages, but we must remain restrained in consumption. It was time for "austerity."

A typical **news-clip** from Britain told of continuing food shortages. It mentioned that all of Europe was drastically under-nourished, with the defeated nations from the war in a particularly bad state. Germans were surviving on a quota of under 1200 calories per day, compared to a normal adult average need of 2500 or more. Britain herself was still doing it tough, with her individual quotas well below those in Australia.

Britain's Food Ministry, Jan 24: The Food Minister, Lord Woolton, said in the House of Lords that it was high time that there was a break in Britain's debilitating austerity.

> Give the people more food and more freedom and they will produce the goods. An extra pound of meat per week would give more stimulus to the miners than arid contemplation of the fact that the public now owns the coal mines.

Lord Henderson, also speaking in the Upper House, gave little hope of **increased** rations. He said that bread rations might yet have to be **reduced further**. There was practically no hope of restoring the bacon ration to three ounces per week in 1947, and the **present ration of two ounces** might have to be reduced.

Lord de L'Isle said it seemed from Government statements that there was no hope of ending rationing for years. Lord Cherwell said that **Britain had less to eat in the first year of peace** than it had in the last year of the war. Now, halfway through the second year of peace, and in spite of bumper harvests in practically every exporting country, people were told they would have to put up with even more meagre rations.

The Ministry announced that the weekly meat ration for 1947 would remain at one shilling and four pence, but the value of **fresh meat** in the ration would be one shilling instead of one shilling and two pence. The remainder would consist of canned meat.

And so the news coverage went on. And on.

MEANWHILE, BACK IN OZ

It was easy for the average young Australian to be optimistic at the start of 1947. Things had gone along pretty well in 1946. Granted there was a lot of grumbling over the fact that all sorts of war-time austerities were still around. For example, rationing and shortages of all sorts of commodities caused constant annoyance. Tens of thousands of soldiers had been poorly repatriated, and were still out of work. Housing was in very short supply, beer was in shorter supply, the number of strikes was increasing, transport services were terrible, and there was no tea left for a cuppa.

Yet despite all this, it would have been the rare person here who felt depressed by all of these things. Hope, they say, springs eternal, and that is what our worthy citizens felt at this time. Hope had been present at the start of 1946 too, but everyone was wiser now and knew it had been unrealistic hope. This time, in 1947, people knew **for sure** that things were going to get better. Despite the fact that **new** rationing books had just been issued, they **knew** that rationing would end soon. Despite the huge backlog in housing, they **knew** that they would all soon get out of their parents' house, and into their own. Everyone **knew** that they would **soon** be able to buy cars and tyres, and rice, and nylon stockings. It was just a matter of time.

The newly elected Government of Ben Chifley said that it too thought all these good things would soon happen. "Anytime now," these wise ones kept saying. "Mind you," they went on to say under their breath, "there might be a few difficulties. We, as a nation, are still desperately short of US dollars, so we cannot afford to buy lots of things we want. Also, we have strong ties to Britain, and that nation is suffering from a severe shortage of everything. We also have to give up our rations for the Mother country. Then, of course, we as a Government want to keep control of prices, and rents, and just about everything, so that a few thousand regulations will still be in force by the end of the year." So the Governmental types, too, were happy that better times would come shortly, though it all might take a tad longer than some people thought.

In all, it was a happy hopeful nation that faced the new year. People were no longer so starry-eyed about what they would do after the war, and were starting to actually do things.

For example, the handsome, gallant ex-soldiers were putting the miseries of military life behind them, and were finding mates from among the lovely young girls who had missed male companions for so long. They were all settling down in marriage, and starting to save, and plan and dream together. And of course, everyone felt lucky in love, so that although they **somehow** learned to make love, many of them did not find out about contraceptives. Thus, without any trouble at all, they did their bit to stimulate the economy via a magnificent Baby Boom.

In my previous book, *Born in 1946*, I was able to talk at length about the way that rationing worked, and point out just how extensive it was, and that it provided real hardships for the average Australian. I also dwelt on the obvious fact that, as a consequence, a sophisticated **black market** for all rationed products had developed, much to the relief of all those who could afford to illegally indulge themselves.

Of course, by the time 1947 came along, you would expect that some or all rationing would be gone, or that the portions allocated would have been increased. After all, the war in the Pacific had finished eighteen months earlier. So that, surely, there could be no rationing of agricultural products. Yes, perhaps rubber and cars and other things made overseas might still be on the list. But not agricultural products. No way.

Well, if you thought that, then you would be, sadly, very wrong. At the start of 1947, and indeed at the end of it, there was virtually no change in the rationing regime. Everyone had just been issued with nice new ration books, with the lovely little coupons all set up in rows. Fifty six bright green coupons for a year's supply of clothes and shoes, and others for butter, and meat, and tea, and sugar, and petrol, and tobacco, and so on. And on top of this there were unofficial impositions on beer, rubber tyres, tractor parts and the like. In short, nothing much had changed.

The Government said there were good reasons for this austerity. **Firstly**, we were short of international currency. And the more we spent, the worse this situation became. It seems that there was some validity to this for petrol and tea and the like, that we imported from overseas. And,

secondly, we owed it to Britain and the Empire to recognise that they were desperately short of food, and to show that we were willing to give up eating freely so that they could have basics, like butter and sugar.

This latter argument was one that, at the time, appealed to most of the population. **We were then still committed to Britain in a big way.** We had been prepared in the war – before the Japanese attack, and after – to send our men and women of all ages to defend England against the Germans, despite the fact that the European war was 12,000 miles from our shores. This type of thinking still prevailed here in 1947. Granted there was much grumbling about short rations, but sacrifice for the sake of Britain was still accepted.

So rationing was here to stay, for the rest of the year, and well beyond for most articles. With rationing came a wonderful ritual that was played out over and over again. Some spokesman or politician would promise that part of rationing would soon be removed. Hopes were raised, a measure of gratitude was supposedly earned by the speaker for his kind announcement, and then, very quietly, some other person would say that due to blah and blah, a reduction was not yet possible. This happened about twice a week, for every week, in 1946, and by 1947 it simply engendered cynicism and frustration within the nation. It was all a wonderful display of vaudeville at its best.

But that's enough talk about the past. **We will now blast off into the future.** After one small detour.

MY RULES IN WRITING

This detour is brief. It just sets out some of my rules in writing this series, and explains why the book is presented in the way that it is.

NOTE. Throughout this book, I reproduce typical Letters from the newspapers. Whenever I do this, I put the text in a different font, and indent it a little, and make the font somewhat smaller. I do not edit the text at all. That is, I do not correct spelling or grammar, and if the text gets at all garbled, I do not correct it. It's just as it was seen in the Papers.

SECOND NOTE. The material for this book, when it comes from newspapers, is reported as it was seen at the time. If the benefit of hindsight over the years changes things, then I **might** record that in my Comments. The info reported reflects matters as they were seen in 1947.

THIRD NOTE. Let me also apologise in advance to anyone I might offend. In a work such as this, it is certain some people will think I got some things wrong. I am sure that I did, but please remember, **all of this is only my opinion**. And really, **my opinion does not matter one little bit in the scheme of things**. I hope you will say **"silly old bugger", shrug your shoulders, and read on**.

So, now we *are* ready. Let's go. Good luck in 1947.

JANUARY NEWS ITEMS

On News Year's Day, **at the Melbourne Cricket Ground,** play between Australia and England started in the five-day Third Test. After the tea-break, a spectator, **"coatless and with his shirt hanging out at the back",** walked onto the field, moved out to the pitch, and insisted on shaking hands with batsman Keith Miller. He wandered around, talking to various fieldsmen....

The umpire accosted the man, and after a warm debate, **collared him, and put him a headlock.** Three policemen arrived, and took the man from the ground....

"Because it was New Year's Day, he was charged only with drunken behaviour."

Find-the-Ball competitions were all the rage with newspapers. The idea was to take an action shot of a moment in a Test Cricket match, while the ball was in flight, and then **to "grey-out" the ball.** The effect was to have the batsman playing a stroke, with the field set about him, but **with no ball in sight....**

This scene was printed in a newspaper, and readers were encouraged to put a cross on the photo guessing at where the centre of the ball would be. The picture was then cut out from the paper and returned with an entry fee of one shilling. The winning prize was one thousand Pounds...

Of course, the ball was nowhere near where you would expect it to be. Profits from the competition went to children's hospitals.

The US had some good news for the world. It talked about progress in the development of the **hydrogen**

bomb, and estimated that they would soon have **a bomb that was 1,000 times more powerful than the old-hat atom bombs** used on Japan. **The world just keeps on getting better and better.**

A spokesman for the British Government bemoaned the fact that **more and more crashes were happening in the aircraft industry**. He said that now that **commercial** airlines were travelling at **the fantastic speed of 100 miles per hour**, greater wing spans and longer runways etc were needed. He lamented the fact that such amenities were not being provided, and that **many lives were being lost around the world.**

Tragedy struck at the Sydney suburb of Canterbury. A boy, just two years old, had been given a dinky for Christmas. He rode it into the yard of a neighbour, and it struck the corner of a small fishpond, four feet square. **He toppled off, into the pond, and drowned.**

In Japan, the divine Emperor has been replaced by the divine General Douglas MacArthur. He sacked over **one million heads and top executives of Companies that created Japan's war machine**....

He issued an edict to that effect one Friday, but this resulted in **the top men resigning and taking up different positions in the same corporation**. So the next Friday, he forbade **this** practice....

MacArthur aims to break up the **centuries-old feudal system** that allowed the formation of a totalitarian state...

At the same time, he reduced **the Emperor's household from 8,900 persons to 1,400.**

YOU LIKE TO TRAVEL - TOO BAD

All of Australia was ready to hit the road. During the war, lots of people had moved all over the world, but most of them were in uniform and carrying a rifle. Many others had travelled throughout the nation, but these had been conscripted to build bridges and roads and airfields. Our womenfolk had journeyed to different regions to work in factories.

But none of these were by choice. In fact, during the war, there was almost no travel for pleasure, or holidays, or to visit far-distant family. **In 1942, for example, annual Christmas holidays for the entire nation were cancelled.** On top of that, petrol was so scarce that once a month you could drive your car readily for a 50-mile trip, but only if you were prepared to walk back. You could book an over-night berth to some capital city, but the chances were that you would get bumped by some wallah with a military brief case.

In short, what I am saying is that no matter how you wanted to travel, **you could not do it.**

So, it was time that all that changed, and everyone could swap places with everyone else, and have a good holiday, and a real break at last.

PETROL AND CARS

At the start of the war, the Commonwealth Oil Board proposed to reduce consumption by the fiendishly cunning device of swamping consumers with propaganda, warning that they should cut back on usage, **or else** rationing would be necessary. It was hoped that voluntary restraint would be encouraged. However, at the first mention of rationing, massive hoarding took place, and the nation was dry within a day.

Later, the Government introduced gas producers as an alternative to petrol. These were devices towed behind the car, like a trailer, that slowly burned a form of charcoal, and in the process produced a combustible gas that was then captured for driving the car. Each car was fitted with half a balloon that sat on the roof of the car, for storing the gas. **The entire set-up was a flop.** Cars needed to be converted from the old to the new system; the whole process of handling the charcoal was messy; the technology was new, and worked only sometimes. To boot, there was no consistent supply of charcoal. More propaganda, exhorting motorists to fit these devices as a patriotic act, was widely distributed. But to little avail. The charcoal burners lingered for a couple of years, but were gone when peace arrived

The level of incompetence was hard to exceed. The Comptroller-General proposed to make the price of petrol so high that rationing could be avoided, but then, no-one would use a car. Another plan was proposed, that petrol should be sold in two colours, blue for commercial vehicles, and red for private cars, with red petrol being substantially more expensive than blue. To differentiate between private and commercial vehicles, all commercial vehicles, including cars, would have the windows blacked out on the passenger side, and a wide strip would be blacked out in front of the passenger's seat. The plan further proposed that inspectors should be given the power to hold up cars at any time to check the colour of the petrol, and that very heavy fines should be imposed for improper use.

These and other grand designs were imposed, and the net effect **was** indeed to reduce petrol consumption for the private motorist who only got one or two short trips a week. Tradesmen and fruitos and the like got more, but large numbers of these brought their horses back out of retirement. Motor transport ground to a halt, except for military vehicles.

After the war, petrol remained severely rationed. The reason was complicated. Britain was disastrously short of US dollars. Everything she did was directed towards earning dollars or to not spending them. But to get petrol, she had to spend them. We of course still followed Britain's economic lead to a large extent, and so we were part of the dollar pool dedicated to **not** spending dollars. And that meant that petrol rationing applied here as well as in England. In fact, so well did we co-operate in this that **our ration here was 30 per cent less than that in Britain** (and New Zealand) at the time, despite our much greater distances.

From 1946, the bungling continued, this time at the highest level. **In 1948, rationing was actually abolished. Later, in 1949, the Federal Government brought it back.** After a long legal battle, the High Court said this was illegal. So the Government went to the people on the issue, and called an election. It lost. The Labor Party was thrown out of office, and made way for 17 years of control by Bob Menzies. His first major act in 1950 was to abolish petrol rationing.

NEWS AND VIEWS ON PETROL AND CARS

Returning to **1947**, the following items show a small range of problems at the time. Note the third item that talks about price controls on all cars. That is, even the process of selling of old cars was controlled, and they could not legally be sold for a different price. Not even to a family member or a friend.

Service Station Association press release: Hundreds of motorists, who were unable to buy petrol at garages in Sydney yesterday, have been left with petrol coupons which are now useless. Some garages will be out of petrol for several days. The General Secretary of the Service Station Association, Mr C. Gregory, said last night that the shortage was the result of the last-minute rush to use up coupons which expired yesterday.

The shortage was becoming more acute at the end of each month. More coupons were in circulation, and many people cashed them even if the petrol was not for immediate use. Customers who had been tipped off by their garage-man to come early for petrol had formed long queues before the garages opened at 9 a.m.

Facilities for the delivery of petrol in bulk to garages were inadequate, because the pool could not supply sufficient tank wagons. A representative of the NRMA said the number of motorists caught on the roads without petrol yesterday was unusually high. Many cars in the Cremorne area had to be towed home.

Letters, J Morris. We can confidently expect that, within a few months, all wartime controls will be lifted, and that drivers will be free to go where they will and purchase all motoring goods on the open market. The dawn of the post-war market has already come, it is said, and soon petrol rationing will be eased, all car parts except batteries will be released from control, and all motorists will be able to have their tyres retreaded without restriction.

That, my friends, is only what we are being told. But the dawn comes in on a watery sky. Innumerable tyres will not stand further work, and even if petrol rationing were lifted to-morrow, the vehicles would not be able to take full advantage of it. New tyres are urgently needed, but it seems that the scene is hardly set for their release to the public. Many thousands of batteries are in the last stages of life and there is no hope of replacing them.

Court report, Melbourne. Christopher Bohrsmann was fined 100 Pounds in the Special Court yesterday for having sold a 1932 Chevrolet car for 400 Pounds, the **fixed price** being 208 pounds. Mr Beaufield (for the Crown) said that a man called Havens had enjoyed an interview with Prices Branch officers, at which bank notes were marked. When the officers entered the office, the notes were found in the safe.

Mr Bohrsmann admitted that he had sold the car for 400 Pounds and that he got a receipt for 208 Pounds. His solicitor said that when Havens first came to him, Bohrsmann had refused to sell, and later persisted in refusing to sell. Havens had pestered him to sell. A week before Christmas, Bohrsmann had broken his arm. When Havens again asked for the car, he agreed to sell at what it had cost him, because he would not be able to drive it for six months, and because of Haven's repeated requests.

Legislative Assembly, April. Transport Minister, Mr O'Sullivan, stated yesterday that more than 7,000 applications to buy utility trucks had been made, while fewer than 150 had become available in the last three months.

In the case of motor cars, the position is little different. Over 15,000 applications, but only 700 cars of all types and makes were allocated each month. Thousands of ex-servicemen are dependent on motor vehicles for their rehabilitation, and so they must be given priority. He said that he was unable to change matters so that other persons could get a better deal.

Petrol pooling. Before the war came, there were eight petrol companies here, each selling petrol under their own well-known names. But, with the war, it was realised that, because no refining was done in Australia, all of these companies were selling the same product. They simply got the petrol off the ships, and took it to their own garages, in effect. There was no need to have petrol identified by brand, and that made the even distribution of the product simpler for rationing purposes. So while garages were still identified by brand, you as a motorist just took what petrol was available.

The petrol companies complained about this. Each of them thought that it could market its own brand better than all the other companies could market theirs. In May, **this petrol pooling was abolished** and each company then sold petrol under its own brand name. A great advertising war broke out, with everyone claiming superiority. But, of course, it was an identical product that was being sold.

Comment. To this very day, the public is subjected to a lot of marketing propaganda from the petrol companies. It appears to me that this public earned its reputation for gullibility back in 1947, and the petrol companies have thrived on it since.

CHIFLEY AND PETROL RATIONING

At the end of 1947, the war had been over for two and a half years. Chifley, during the war, had been Treasurer of the Commonwealth, and had picked up all the theories that economists were then prone to. One of these was that the way out of financial problems was not to spend. Nowadays, in 2020, there are many people who hold the opposite view, that if you do spend, you stimulate the economy and break out of the debt cycle.

In any case, Chifley saw that Britain and Australia were desperately short of US dollars, and **so he decided to manage this by not spending them**. And nowhere was his determination so obvious as in the case of petrol spending. There were constant cries from the whole community that petrol rationing should be abolished as it had been in most other countries, that it was more severe here than in Britain. But Chifley held his ground, through the rationing fiasco and then elections of the 1949 year.

Chifley, to me, had a belief that if he did what he perceived to be the right thing, then the populace would come to recognise that it was right, and in the long run vote for him next time. But not everyone agreed that all of his actions were right, and certainly only the staunchest Laborite thought he was right on petrol. So he stayed with his petrol stance to the very end, as we shall see in later books.

COULD YOU BUY AND RUN A CAR?

Suppose you had enough petrol for a good motoring trip.

That probably means that you were sufficiently rich to buy on the black market. Suppose you had enough petrol, and suppose that your tyres were still in one piece. Could you take a long motoring trip?

Of course you could. And a jolly good trip it might be. And it would be all the more precious because so few of your friends and neighbours could do the same.

Though there were a few hazards. The roads were all terrible. Maintenance of non-military roads had not been high on the public agenda during the war. Then there was the problem that almost all roads were unsealed, and also single-laned with no passing lanes. If you got behind a slow truck, you would be stuck there for the duration.

There were also plenty of **punts** to bring joy. **But only in the daytime.** Across most of Australia, there are inland rivers that flow to the sea. Some of these were blessed by bridges, but many of them were not. For example, on the Pacific Highway from Sydney to Brisbane, there were five rivers that needed a punt to cross. You might be better to head for Broken Hill, but you would need to carry all your own petrol in the boot.

Still, you might want to buy your own car. Could you do this?

Of course you could. But it might take a while. Companies like Ford from the US, and Morris from Britain, were offering a wide range of glossy new cars. They were for sale at a price that the working man could not afford, especially before the advent of Hire Purchase. But for the sons of the rich, that was no real problem. Still, as the car salesmen very quietly pointed out when pressed, **delivery time to Australia would be at least one year, and probably closer to three**. Maybe by then there would be enough petrol to use them freely.

NEWS AND VIEWS

Booze and Gaspers. An official announcement pointed out that next month, it would not be possible to provide the full ration of tobacco for persons entitled to get same. For that month, the amount allocated would be 75 per cent of the nominal ration.

A spokesman for Tooth's Brewery said that ample beer supplies are not in sight. He could not predict yet when satisfactory production would be available.

Butter. Also, to add cheer to those who thought that butter rationing should have ended, there is this little note from the **British Dominions Office**.

> Britain has acceded to a Canadian request for 6,000 tons of Australian butter. Most of Australia's surplus butter is exported to Britain. However, Canada now is short of the product and needs to import large quantities to maintain its fat ration at six ounces per week. Britain, by comparison gets a per person ration of three ounces of butter per week, and three ounces of margarine, and one ounce of cooking fat.

> The British Government has reached a difficult decision that it will pass on **6,000 tons of Australian butter to Canada** to provide some relief to their temporary shortage. Australia has agreed to this shipment.

It is not all bad news. The Department of Agriculture's. **broom millet** specialist said yesterday that reports of the failure of the season's crop on the Richmond River were greatly exaggerated. The drought had certainly limited production and had disappointed growers, who had expected bigger yields, but the total output in the State should be up to the average of the last ten years. He added that manufacturers had a substantial carry-over from the last year.

Comment. In the days when most housewives did not have vacuum cleaners or when most of the few existing cleaners had given up the ghost long ago, news of the availability of brooms was big news indeed.

Indian View of White Australia. Mahatma Ghandi was replying to the question "should rich men give up their private property to create a trust for the common good?" He replied that when a person owned more than his share of assets, then **he became a trustee for all of God's people** and would be judged by the manner in which he executed that trust.

He went on to say that Australia was a nation of rich people (compared to India) and that by introducing **policies that refused entry to coloured people, it was betraying that trust.** If countries such as Australia did not change, then a war, more violent than the last two wars, would be likely.

Announcement from Vatican City. The Pope has waived observance of the 40-days Lenten fast for those particularly affected by the world's food crisis. He said the fast could not be observed by "those of the faithful whose present circumstances in Lenten period make even normal living extremely difficult."

Comment. I want to put this in perspective. In my **1946** book, I reported that hundreds of millions of Europeans were living on a ration of 750 calories per day. The average Australian intake is over 2500 per day. To make any suggestion that these poor unfortunate Europeans could cut down on their eating was, to say the very least, crass.

FEBRUARY NEWS ITEMS

Champion race horse, **Bernborough,** has laryngitis. He arrived in Sydney from Melbourne, on board the *Wangaratta*, with the ailment. It is expected that it will be better by the time he reaches **his destination of the United States in a few weeks**....

The race horse **had previously won 15 consecutive races** with huge weights, including the prestigious Doomben Cup carrying almost 11 stone. **He will perform at studs in the US. His new owner will be Louis B Mayer**, of MGM fame.

The last of the American General Infantry (**G.I.'s**) **left the European zone** on February 2nd. At the peak of the war, **there were 5 million G.I.'s in that zone.**

Hamberg, Germany. **Five women and six men were sentenced to death by hanging** for their part in committing **war-time atrocities at the Ravensbruck** Womens' Concentration Camp....

Thousands of prisoners were drowned, gassed, tortured, poisoned, shot, gassed or frozen to death, **mostly in the name of science.**

Riotous living in Canberra. Immigration Minister Arthur Calwell was refused entry to the dining room at the top-notch Canberra Hotel **because he was not wearing a tie**. He borrowed one from a waiter....

Another gentleman, a delegate from the South Sea Conference, was refused entry because he arrived at the dining room **two minutes late for the 7 o'clock sitting**.

He went to **the bar** for a drink, and found that it too **was closed**. He tried to order **breakfast in his bed-room**. The hotel did not offer that service....

He wondered publicly how such a hotel could claim to be "**of international standard**". Little did he know that most of **our hotels at that time were as bad or worse**.

Arthur Calwell was in the news again next day. He announced that a large liner, the *Aquitania*, would be chartered by the Australian Government to **bring migrants to Australia from Europe**. This was considered a good thing because the shortage of shipping was preventing trade and travel with overseas nations....

What was more questionable was that the ship normally carried 2,000 passengers, but he will have it outfitted so that it can carry over 3,000. He expected that migrants would be so anxious to get here that "they would be prepared to **put up with conditions at a lower standard than normal.**" This was especially true for single men....

He did not dwell on how **families with children would fare on the six-week journey**.

Don Bradman got a duck in the Fifth Test against England last Saturday. This was disappointing, because it **was his last Test, and it left his average at 99.9.**

Melbourne, Sydney, Townsville and Darwin will have **international airports in a few years**. This will involve building longer runways and adding terminal buildings , including baggage facilities. **There was no talk in those innocent days of security measures.**

McKELL AS GOVERNOR GENERAL

The **nominal** term of office for a Governor General is five years, though in practice it can be quite different from that. Sometimes, under unusual circumstances, a person might linger longer or shorter. For example, General the Right Honourable Alexander Gore Arkwright Hore-Ruthven, otherwise known as Baron Gowrie, started in 1936, and was due to serve only three years. Then his replacement, the Duke of Kent, was prevented from taking up his post because of the war, in which he lost his life. So the Baron actually stayed on for a total of nine years, until 1945, when he was replaced by the King's brother, the Duke of Gloucester. And that dignitary stayed for only two years as the King's representative in this land.

As it became obvious that the term of the Duke was coming to an end, some of the natives started to get restless. It was, by then, the official policy of federal Labor and of most of the State governments, that future GGs should be Australian born. Curtin had drawn a lot of criticism for appointing the Duke of Gloucester, but he argued that in 1945, **with Australia pressing the British for their help in the Pacific war**, having the King's brother here was a shrewd move. But, in late 1946, a return to Labor policy was on the cards. After all, said Labor, we have a Labor Government, and the Duke, while we respect him fully, is scarcely able to make representation on behalf of the people of Australia, because he is not a citizen of this fine nation. So pressure mounted, especially from Labor ranks, to appoint an Australian Governor General.

This was not the first time that such a measure was contemplated. In 1931, for the very first time, a local boy got the job. Though Sir Isaac Isaacs was anything but a boy. He had in fact been for many years a distinguished judge, and was at the time Chief Justice of the High Court. The Labor Prime Minister, Scullin, back in office in 1929 after a long period in opposition, brought with him a determination that the GG must be an Australian. So he put up the name of Isaacs to George V, and he put up no one else's. This forced the King to accept Isaacs, a decision he did not wish to make. But Scullin had been careful to select a distinguished person, one **who was not associated with partisan politics**, and who it could be argued, would be free to act impartially in the event of adjudicating in controversial matters.

In 1947, Chifley thought otherwise. He thought that the GG's job was **really one for the boys**, a position thoroughly suitable as a reward for a retiring Labor politician. It mattered not whether the King liked the appointee, or even whether he knew him. So again, only one name was proposed – by cable, with no discussion – and it was that of William McKell, **the recently retired Labor Premier of NSW.**

Of course, not every one agreed with this offhand approach. Menzies, then the Leader of the Opposition, argued that the GG was the trusted personal representative of the King in this country, and was not the **political** representative of the Government. And therefore that great weight should be given to His Majesty's wishes in this matter. He also argued that if ex-politicians were appointed, along party lines, then each time a party went out of office the GG would have to go too. And that would lead to the office of the GG being degraded to an absurdity.

Menzies in turn was faced with the counter offensive that he was proposing a system that would guarantee that "Australians need not apply." He, in reply, argued that the most obvious course of action was to appoint someone who the King knew personally and felt he could trust. Given the fact that the King lived in Britain, then it seemed most likely that suitable candidates would come from that nation. If someone from Australia **did** gain the King's approval, then Menzies could see no objection, provided that this person was not straight out of a political party.

Still, Menzies protested in vain, and the appointment went ahead. A few people supported the decision.

Letters, R Trickett. It appears that the critics of Mr McKell as Governor General are more concerned about the **social qualifications** of the holder of the position rather than qualifications of ability and experience.

The Premier of NSW has shown outstanding ability during his term of office, and I am yet to be convinced he is lacking in the necessary social qualifications also. I am sure that with all his experience he will uphold the dignity of the office.

As a result of efficient management, the McKell government has been able to extend benefits that will bring cheer and happiness, comfort and contentment to all citizens. It will be time enough to be critical and fault finding when circumstances warrant.

Chifley argued in favour, not surprisingly.

I feel confident that he will discharge the duties of his high office with ability and dignity. His appointment follows the precedent established in Australia in the

1930's, and in South Africa, in which places the distinguished public service of native-born citizens has been recognised.

The President of the ACTU rallied to the cause. Mr P. Clarey said "All fair-minded Australians wish Mr McKell every success. His outstanding services to NSW fit him in every way for the position of GG."

On the other hand, **most people were against it**. The reaction from the nation's press was totally unfavourable. The *Sydney Morning Herald* (*SMH*) bemoaned the fact that the decision had been leaked widely for a month before it was made public. But more important was its criticism of the appointment of a person who was still an active politician, and who would always be subject to claims that he was politically biased in everything he did. It said that Australians, regardless of their political affiliations, were "astounded and shocked". And the whole affair was made worse by the fact that Chifley had persisted even after the King had been made aware that the appointment was unacceptable to a very great number of Australians. Nothing alters the fact that "a serious blow has been struck at the one institution which signifies the unity of the British people."

Brisbane's *Courier Mail* said the appointment was shameful because, in pushing their mean Party line, those responsible had robbed Australia of a very real protection. This was to remove a corrupt and dictatorial Government, if ever it was necessary. The move to appoint McKell can only destroy public confidence in the impartiality and complete detachment that is needed for the King's representative.

Bob Menzies, of course, was very critical. Apart from his ideological pronouncements on **the process** of the appointment expressed above, he had a lot to say about the specifics.

It is a shocking and humiliating appointment. It constitutes the most deplorable incident in the Government's growing record of political jobbery. One is forced to the conclusion that it is expressly designed to lower the GG's status in significance and esteem, and so weaken our links with Great Britain and the British Crown.

Letters poured in to the newspapers, raising all sorts of points.

Letters, Frank Everingham. The insinuation by Mr Frazer that **criticism** of McKell's promotion is disloyal to the Throne can be dismissed with contempt.

No possible ground can be found in any aspect of McKell's political life to excuse his elevation to this august position, with its tradition of impartiality. No political careerist of any sort has ever, and does not now, deserve the State emolument of 10,000 Pounds per annum, tax free.

The appointment carries a vague but definite suggestion to every man who donned a uniform in two world wars. That is, it suggests that political careerism is of greater service to the nation than the battlefield.

Letters, J Wright. As GG, Mr McKell automatically becomes Commander-in-Chief of the Armed Forces of the Commonwealth, and patron of several ex-Servicemen's organisations. Could anything be more ironic?

Had names agreeable to the majority of people in Australia been submitted to the King, in addition to

McKell's, I have no doubt that the latter would still be **Premier of NSW**.

Letters, L Parker. Actually, Australia is having a taste of the state of affairs prevailing in republican States in which the head of state enjoys the respect of one section, but hostility, either passive or violent, from the rest.

To all who have enjoyed the British serenity of a non-party head of State, the present conditions should provide a useful warning. Let us hope that future Governments will not repeat the experiment.

Letters, O Bissett. The other aspects of the GG's duties are semi-official and social though, unhappily, many may not think so. These are of considerable importance to the ordinary men and women of Australia in all walks of life.

It would be idle to suggest that McKell has **the training, background or personality** to perform these duties with any satisfaction to the public. If the appointment goes ahead, the office would be bereft of its main function and justification.

In the past, a feature of considerable importance has been the knowledge and culture brought to us from overseas by the **wives** of the various GG's, their high standard of public spirit and service, and the inspiring ability they have displayed. I do not suppose that any woman in any walk of life has done more for Australia than Lady Gowrie, or given such inspiration as she gave to all who met her.

Is this all to be thrown away in order to satisfy the ambitions of a humdrum party politician?

Comment. The above two Letters contained veiled hints that the McKells were not always considered to be refined by British standards.

Letters, A Baille. In 1913, a Mr Piddington was appointed to the High Court of Australia. After emphatic protests from the legal profession, he resigned from the position. Mr McKell would likewise show himself to be a big man if he had the decency and principle to refuse the post offered to him.

Letters, C.L.R. What better honour and more befitting compliment than to install Field Marshall Montgomery as the new Governor General. He is a most popular man, and an ex-serviceman. I suggest that we Australians organise a petition, and I am sure that many thousands would sign it.

Letters, ELECTOR. I have written to various authorities suggesting the best way of protesting over Mr McKell is for the entire Opposition to resign. This will force a new election and give the man in the street a chance to show his displeasure.

A few days before McKell was sworn in, Menzies added a little threat that doubtless McKell noted **without** much glee. Menzies said, rather vaguely, in Parliament that **an incoming Government** should **rescind** some notoriously party appointment, and appoint someone far above politics, and that would restore the dignity of the post. Outside the Parliament, when asked to be quite specific, he said "I thought I dealt with that aspect with great care. Whatever inference you might read into it will no doubt be right." Perhaps it was an empty threat, but it doubtless registered with the GG.

The inauguration ceremony went as well as could be expected. The normal pomp and circumstance was present and the ceremony was as grand as official functions can be. However, many Liberal politicians did not attend, and even a third of Labor politicians stayed away. This latter group indicated that they had some House duties to attend to, but observers think that unlikely. One Labor politician who did attend was Rowley James, the long-standing Member for Hunter, who distinguished himself by calling out "Good on Yer, Bill" as McKell entered.

When McKell left office, it was Menzies' turn to make an appointment. He did it properly, according to his standards. The Queen asked him, "with a twinkle in her eye", how he proposed to do it. He suggested that he, and the Queen, and Lord Bobbety Salisbury should each write down their own three suggestions, and then pool them. Salisbury was, according to Menzies, a person "who knows everybody of consequence, and with great judgment." The Queen apparently liked this very much, and said she thought it quite a charming way to solve constitutional problems.

Two days later, the three envelopes were opened. The first name out of each was Sir William Slim, and so their decision was unanimous. So Menzies was able to do it his way. He got a fine English gentleman and soldier, who was known to the Queen, and unconnected with politics.

Of course, looking back from 2017, all of this has changed so much. The Liberals did later appoint a **serving** politician in the person of Paul Hasluck, and since then Bill Hayden (Labor) and Lord Casey (Liberal) also accepted the post.

Now, it is the custom to appoint only Australians, and it seems that distinguished persons in civilian walks of life, or the military, are hot favourites. But there is little doubt that any appointment of a Britisher, from the nobility or elsewhere, would be abhorrent to all but the most fervent monarchist.

OTHER MODES OF LOCAL TRAVEL

If you have given up on travel by car, and you just wanted to get to work in the city, what about a bus or tram? It is safe to say that both of these were unpleasant because they were always crowded, uncomfortable and uncertain. The bus conductors and their few women equivalents were quite often little martinets. "Move down the aisle" they shouted. Or "get off the back platform" of double-decker buses, or "get off the running boards" of trams. Somehow they managed to look disheveled in their State-provided uniforms, even with a generous cleaning allowance.

But there were other problems with trams.

The following letter gives some idea of the joys of tram travelling.

Court report, Mar 12: Twenty-six men were fined one Pound each at Central Court yesterday for footboard riding on trams at the week-end. One other was fined ten shillings, and three did not appear and forfeited their recognizance. Fred Templeton, aged 36, who was fined ten Shillings, told the S.M. that he had stepped on to the running boards to allow a passenger to alight, and had been unable to get back inside. Mr Goldie said there were mitigating circumstances in his case, but footboard riding was dangerous, and would have to stop.

Letters, Billy Budd. I hate seeing tram conductors getting a fare, and then giving half of it back, and pocketing the rest, without issuing a ticket. It might get them a bit of pocket-money, and the passenger might get a penny or two for the risk, but it deprives the rest of us of our legitimate revenue. Why can I always see this, and yet the Inspectors cannot. Are they blind, or are they in on the racket?

Letters, CONDUCTOR, Waverley Depot. The general opinion of your correspondence seem to be that heavy transport losses are due, in the main, to the "sharp practices of our transport men."

I assure them that the majority of us conductors value our souls far more highly than a few pence. The few men who indulge in the form of self-help mentioned should be referred to in the past tense, as none remain in the employ of the Department for more than a brief period. In any case, the losses due to this dishonesty would be small, indeed, compared with the many thousands lost annually because of the sharp practices of so many of the travelling public.

In my list of "hates" I include, **first**, the North Shore scaler, who boards the tram at the Quay, and travels one or two stops, and hops off before I get to him. **Second**, women who cannot hear my voice saying "fares please," and who eventually rummage through their bags and then come up with a pound note. **Third**, men who take up their position at the front or rear entrance and who make a quick flit if I come near them.

CATCH A TRAIN?

City trains were dirty, wind-swept, late or cancelled, and crowded. The seats were often ripped, the army of station attendants was rude, ticket-buying took forever, the doors would not shut in cold wet weather, and often would not open when the train stopped. Apart from that, they were fine.

Country trains were not as good. Note that there were still First Class and Second Class carriages, as well as smoker and non-smoker carriages and compartments. But they suffered from all the complaints listed above, and a few more.

For example, there were often a few girl employees wandering the train offering food and drink from trolleys. The prices were exorbitant, but the outstanding feature was the staleness of the food. How the Railways managed their supply chain so that their pies were **always** a week old is a mystery. How their pots of tea got so cold, even on hot days, is another.

Another example was the manner in which luggage was handled. Every long-distant traveller in those days had a number of ports. They could not fit into the normal over-crowded carriages, and there was a special luggage van at the rear of the train for the ports. This extra service came with a guarantee that either your port would be put ashore at the wrong station, or that it would be so battered that you would scarcely recognise it. As part of the Railway's attempts to win the hearts of their paying customers, this service was provided free for the first two ports, with an extra charge for excess.

What I am saying is that long distance travel by train, especially laden with ports or children, was difficult and unpleasant.

But there was some hope for train travellers in the City of Sydney.

Premier's Press releases, Mar 23: Work will begin immediately on construction of the Eastern Suburbs Railway. The vast task will take seven years. Details of the project were announced by the Premier Mr McKell, and the Minister for Transport, Mr O'Sullivan last night. The scheme embraces the long-mooted Eastern

Suburbs Railway, new services to the South–Eastern and Southern suburbs, and additional tracks around Redfern to relieve congestion.

This was another one of those vote-catchers that were glibly offered to the public. In fact, **this** railway was promised more often, over the years, than any other item in the newspapers. It opened finally on June 23, 1979. That is **thirty two years after this announcement was made**.

Comment. My above comments on public transport were, shall we say, robust. Some might even say they were scathing but, because **I do not like to scathe in public**, I would disagree. In any case, let me add that there was a good reason why these systems of travel were so bad.

It was that, by the end of the war, everything in the nation was run-down or broken. It would take several fortunes and many years to get transport up to scratch, and the nation was just starting on this. One thing that hampered this was the fact that so many public employees involved **had jobs for life**, and this made them impervious to providing service to customers.

But there were others employees who were as frustrated by the deficiencies as I obviously was. It took a lot of time and a lot of money to change the systems and attitudes to get them up to a satisfactory level. And, **often**, this has been done. **Certainly things are much better now than in 1947.**

MARCH NEWS ITEMS

A farmer near the NSW town of Berry drove his tractor over a snake and cut off its head. He got off to have a look, and picked up a snake. But **it was the wrong snake, and it bit him**. The live snake escaped, and the farmer survived.

Scotland Yard has asked the Sydney, Melbourne and Adelaide **Museums** to send an expert to London to **identify dead and preserved butterflies** that have been found in a house. The authorities suspect they were stolen from Australia. These three museums have respectively reported **1,500, 825, and 603 such butterflies as being stolen**.

March 3rd. New tea coupons will be issued nation-wide today. No one in those days cared if coffee was rationed or not.

150 white galahs were sent by rail from the country to the Sydney city station of Stanmore**.** The consignee refused to pay for them. **Station employees released them** so they could get food and water, but they settled in the waiting room at the station....

They **screeched and fluttered and "dropped" a great deal**, and ate the light fittings and anything in the room and on the station. After a day, **a bird dealer crated them and took them away** with the hope of selling them for five Shillings each.

The *London Times* **newspaper advertised a circus for sale** in the personal column. The circus could be sent to any country "including Australia". It includes five dancing elephants, eight Bengal tigers, camels, zebras, baboons, and sea lions, and all Big Top equipment....

The famous German circus has **been stranded in Sweden by regulations since the war**, and is now forced to sell. **The price should be good if you are interested.**

Australia will make a gift of 25 million Pounds to Britain. The Government said that it was conscious of the great financial problems that the Mother Country was facing, and it wanted to help. It was impossible to increase our food exports further, but instead it reduced the debt that Britain owed to Australia by 25 million....

The giving of this gift was accepted by Australians without demur, and **it showed again how strong the bonds were between ourselves and the Brits**.

Jobs for the boys and girls. A gentleman by the name of **Harold Holt** stated in the House of Representatives that the Department of Post War Reconstruction was ripping the covers off reports from Britain and the USA, and re-covering them, **presenting the reports as if they were their own work**. He said that they were **pretending that they were very busy** so that **their jobs would be retained**....

It was well known that thousands of Public Servants, both State and Federal, who occupied **cushy jobs and wielded great power during the war, were anxious that such jobs should never be abandoned**. Harold Holt was one of the first to publicly come out and talk about this. Needless to say, there were many persons who denied his allegations.

REGULATIONS GALORE

During the war, **rationing was not the only bugbear** that the nation had to put up with. There were regulations, and prohibitions and controls, and authorities, and penalties, and so on, ad nauseum. Think of all the rules and regulations that beset us now, and multiply them by some big factor. Granted, most of them **were** necessary. Some of them turned out to be fatuous and otherwise a waste of time. But no one knew **that** at the time, because there simply was **no text book that set out what to do if a war came**. So for good or for bad, if this nation wanted to go to war – and apparently it did – it had to accept restrictions on its freedoms, and roll with the punches that these regulations delivered.

After the war, the general population wanted these freedoms restored as quickly as sensibly possible. As it turned out, people were quite prepared to be patient, and gradual progress was enough to keep them happy. Governments, both State and Federal, on the other hand, were reluctant to release the reins. Perhaps it was because they saw the nation going to the dogs if economic forces were suddenly unleashed. Perhaps it was vested interests in the Canberra and other bureaucracies. Probably it was a genuine fear that the nation would spend too much currency, and that the dollar pool for Mother England would be depleted. Whatever the reason, there was a lot of governmental foot-dragging.

The biggest scuff mark was made by the Federal Government itself in relation to the timing of **the arrival of peace.** The National Security Act – the source of many of the regulations – was by law set to expire six months after "his Majesty ceases to be engaged in war." So it would appear clear cut: we had stopped fighting, so surely that meant we were at peace. This view was apparently strengthened when Dr. Evatt formally fixed September 3 1945 as the date that **hostilities ceased** with Japan. But then came the double-speak. He pointed out that this would not affect the duration of the National Security Act, because this was dependent on the **formal declaration of peace.**

So what we had here was the proposition that we had stopped hostilities, but we were still not at peace. And we would not be at peace until we issued a declaration saying that we were. And by mid-1946, the Government would give no indication as to when this might be. By then, the Coal Owners Association and the Real Estate Institute started to exert real pressure on Government, and challenged in the Courts. These matters were thus tied down, and so for the rest of 1946, and into 1947, we were somewhere between peace and war – **that** should be clear enough for anyone....

So the Commonwealth hung on to its powers, slowly relinquishing them one at a time, under pressure. The small sample of restrictions below illustrates a handful of the many. Some stem from government, and others come from the staid nature of society itself. I expect you will see the frustrations that were caused; the question I ask myself is whether the current sets of regulations are any better. After all, no one **then** needed 100 points to open a bank account. And anyone could change their address for officialdom without signing an affadavit. And people could get on to planes without removing their shoes first. Perhaps there is a law somewhere that no matter what happens, the tail will always wag the dog.

In passing, I point out that there was **a deeper, more permanent set of restraints imposed on the population, by the population itself**. These were the outcome of history, social mores, acculturation, and an endless stream of other possible social sources. The end result was a society that lived with many restraints. For example, patrons at theatres were expected to stand at the beginning of performances for the rendition of *God Save the King*. This was not a regulation, but woe betide anyone who sat down. Then there was the tribal custom of warfare between Catholics and Masons, with their constant battling over such matters as who should get a railway porter's job. Trivial maybe now, but deadly serious then.

Catholics were also locked into another time-honoured custom, this time one that flew in the face of Protestant churches, over the matter of mixed marriages. Both parties conjured up volumes of rules forbidding this iniquitous practice, and at the same time fostered endless arguments about whether the Duke of Windsor was legally married to the divorced Mrs Simpson.

As another example, consider school clothing. At all the "better schools", girls were not seen in public without their gloves. At the "best" boys' schools, the straw boater was considered an essential educational tool, without which no boy could possibly learn Pythagorus. Vestiges of this still remain at these schools, but looking back we can see that the attitude then was, let's say, different .

As remarkable as these above restraints now seem, they were important in setting the standards by which people lived. But, back to this Chapter's theme of looking at some government regulations.

Regulation of share trading. Throughout the war, the value of shares sold on the nation's stock exchanges had been fixed by a formula that (roughly) set a standard price and then said the movement above that was limited to a small set amount. In effect, the prices were fixed, with just a little leeway for a small gain. Of course, if the share fell, it could be bought cheaper, and then increased capital gain would be possible. But only up to the defined limit.

Obviously, this system was likely to not only curb speculation, but any form of welcome entrepreneurial activity at all. By 1946-47, many large holders were simply not trading, knowing full well that Government must soon relax the limits, and that prices would rise as they did so.

Capel Court Investments, Mr Stanisford Ricketson. The system of ceiling price limits operate in Australia, but not elsewhere. There never was at any time any financial or economic justification for ceilings on shares. The war efforts of Great Britain, the USA, Canada, South Africa and New Zealand did not suffer through lack of them. The open market prices in New Zealand and London for some Australian stocks are higher than the official price limit here.

As it turned out, the very day this letter was published, the upper limits on the trading prices of 69 shares were increased. In the next few months, all the remaining shares received the same treatment. This does not mean that there were no upper limits; just that they were increased some percentage points. However it began a process that lasted almost two years, and happily, by then the artificial limits were gone for good.

Rental regulations. The worst of the worst of the regulations related to houses and flats. In about 1941, the Commonwealth and the States brought down regulations that said the rent on houses and flats would be fixed at 1941 levels. This was to prevent inflation of rents in a period when no new ones would be built. This seemed sensible enough, but by 1947, the regulations were still in place, and showed no signs of being relaxed.

That meant that tenants were still paying the same prices as in 1941, despite six years of inflation. **This was great for tenants, but terrible for landlords.** But the **number of tenants far exceeded the number of landlords**, so our politicians decided it would be wise to not raise rents.

Can you believe it, but it was **not until about 1967** that these regulations were removed in most States. This of course meant that **no investor would finance the building of new dwellings** and this was a partial cause of the housing shortage that lasted for two decades after the war.

Another set of regulations that hurt was the virtual ban on selling your real estate. Of course, no one said that this was the case, but the administration of so doing was prohibitive. For example, the buyer and seller had to agree a price, and send it off by mail to Canberra. There it would be compared to the Valuer General's guess at the real value, and then 10 other regulations would be invoked to prevent the sale. Each exchange of letters took two months, and by the time a decision was reached, the time involved would be two years. By which time, something would have changed, and the bid would not still be standing.

Between the restrictions on rents, and the those on selling, the **real estate industry was crippled for the war years**.

War Agricultural Committees dissolved. These Committees in NSW were officially disbanded this week. The Land Editor of the *SMH* commented favourably on them and said that they did a good job under difficult circumstances. On the other hand, many farmers thought they were interfering busybodies, and quite a few added that they were intent simply on furthering their own interests. In any case, they did have remarkable powers, in theory at least. These will become apparent as you read the item. And so, too, will the scope for abuse in small communities.

Letters, Brian Bright. What is to take their place? With all their limitations, they did an excellent job of work in wartime. Most of their duties were onerous, many thoroughly distasteful and at times, local influence made it difficult to secure the efficiency and impartiality so necessary to succeed.

Their chief duties were advice and direction, neither of which make for popularity, and as they lacked executive power in themselves, it was sometimes difficult to achieve as much as most of them hoped to.

The committees were vitally important links in the general scheme of planned agriculture, and as the Chairman of each was an officer of the Department of Agriculture, it was possible to correlate and pass on that experience without more interference than was necessary in the working of the individual properties. Even then, their work was often described as bureaucratic regimentation.

Their main objective was to equalise the disabilities from which all farmers and graziers suffered during the war, and on the whole, the committees did it well.

Anybody charged with the duty of saying which farmer was more entitled than his neighbour to retain his labour, better transport, more machinery, additional petrol, or priority in spare parts was bound to become unpopular with those who got least, but it was a wartime job that simply had to be done.

Regulations for policemen. Throughout the war, most police officers in many states were not permitted to join the military services. They were classified as being employed in **Essential Services**, and they needed to stay at their civilian posts. After the war, they came up against a different type of problem. The Police Department did provide accommodation for its officers, but with a restriction.

News item: Abolition of the ban which prevented policemen from **marrying within three years of enlisting** was demanded by the Police Association yesterday. It also protested strongly against the Department's withholding of a married man's **allowances** for three years in the few cases in which relaxation of this rule had been allowed. W Madden, of No 14 Branch, said it was impudence to tell anyone he could not marry. The only reason the Police Department did it was to save money.

Mr Bullock, No 15 Branch, said the Department should let the ban be known when they were recruiting. Many young men would not join if they knew of it. The Department was recruiting a number of returned soldiers who had be given no chance to marry for five years, and it would be ridiculous to bar their marriage.

Regulations on vegetable pricing. Growers prices for a further group of vegetables would not be controlled after today, Mr Dedman has announced. The vegetables concerned are beetroot, cauliflower, silver beet, cabbage, celery, turnips, carrots and parsnips. Mr Dedman said that they were additional to the items removed from price control in February.

The relaxation would apply only to growers' prices. Sellers prices are still controlled by the Prices Commission. New orders fixing maximum margins at approximately the rate now in operation would be issued.

Regulation of prices generally. A special investigation squad of the Prices Branch yesterday began an intensive search through greengrocers' shops, hotels, and guest houses for prices violations. Mr F. Herlihy, Deputy Prices Commissioner, said that the investigation had been going on for some time, but that a "blitz" was now being made. Many complaints had been made about greengrocers' prices and proprietors' tariffs.

About 200 hotels will be checked. Present prices will be compared with those of 1942. Tariff charges, especially those for children, had crept above regulation limits. He had visited the South Coast last week, and had found no boarding-house obeying the regulations.

First move by the investigation squad would be in resorts such as Bowral, Moss Vale, Bundanoon, and Katoomba. Mr Herlihy said he was not looking for prosecutions, but unless violators of the regulations adjusted their prices, they would be charged.

The President of the NSW Fruit Shopkeepers' Association said that claims of overcharging were unreasonable. He challenged Mr Herlily to tell him how he could determine retail prices on current wholesale prices, when every wholesaler was charging his own particular price on the market. The solution lay in enforcing the regulation compelling agents to issue dockets with their sales.

The Minister for Post War Reconstruction said today he had no intention of lifting the restrictions on meal prices. He said that a better meal could be bought for a given sum in Australia than anywhere else. He rejected the suggestion that the meals available were a deterrent to the tourist trade.

Deputy Prices Commissioner, Mr F. Herlihy, said yesterday that the large and well-known Sydney hotels, Australia, Ushers, and Carlton, would be prosecuted for unauthorised price increases. He alleged that these hotels have added **a service charge** of one shilling and sixpence. This was on top of the **standard meal charge** of four Shillings for lunch, and five Shillings for tea. One manager said that regulations had been lifted on **the number of courses** that could be offered, but at the same time, the standard prices had not been increased. "How can they expect us to provide more at the same price?"

Mr Herlihy went on to say that his inspectors had in one case found a clear overcharge for oysters, which had sold for an extra nine pence over the standard price of two shillings and sixpence. **Such offences would be taken very seriously**, he said. "**These hotels cannot just make their own decisions on pricing.** They must be subject to the law."

Sewing machines? Surely not. The gazettal of an order fixing **maximum prices** for 122 types of **used** domestic sewing machines was announced today by the

Commonwealth Prices Commissioner, Mr McCarthy. The maximum price for sewing machines not listed is five Pounds.

The notice requires any person offering a used domestic sewing machine for sale, other than by auction, to attach or display a ticket or label showing the selling price. Any person who advertises a used sewing machine for sale must include the name and address of the advertiser, the make and description of the machine, the maximum fixed price, and the price he intends to accept for it.

Regulations on things unmentionable. Talks relating to sex matters and venereal disease should not be **broadcast** from National or commercial stations, stated the ninth report of the Parliamentary Committee on Broadcasting, tabled in Parliament today.

Remember radio listeners' licences.   The Postmaster General, Senator Nash, said to-day that it was hoped that it would be practicable to give broadcast listeners' licences at half cost to Service pensioners.

Regulations for hatmakers, Post-War Reconstruction. The Minister, Mr Dedman, announced a new deal for hatmakers. He noted that a voluntary agreement with hatmakers had now ceased, and makers were now free to create new designs.

However, no new **styles** are expected for quite a while, because of the current ongoing difficulty with production of the **current** styles. A Melbourne hat manufacturer last night said that his company would have to reduce production of the existing lines, and that creation of new lines was out of the question.

Enforcing regulations or religious bias? City Council Inspectors yesterday questioned people in the city streets who were advertising a forthcoming meeting of Jehovah's Witnesses in the Town Hall. Names and addresses, of men bearing sandwich-board posters and women with leaflets pinned to their dresses, were taken. The Town Clerk, Mr Roy Hendy, said last night that distributing leaflets or advertising of meetings by people in city streets were offences, and if inspectors found people doing so, they would be prosecuted.

> **Letters, A Barker.** On Saturday, citizens were arrested and charged with traffic offences relating to the carrying of placards and distributing of handbills relating to a public meeting.
>
> It appears to me that such actions strike at the very roots of freedom, the freedom of public gathering. This precious liberty, fought for and won by courageous Englishmen, is now obliquely attacked by such prosecutions. Most of our freedoms have been won by idealists battling against prejudice and the status quo. These idealists, usually rich only in courage, must resort to the cheapest means of contacting the public from whom they seek support.
>
> If the right to distribute handbills is denied, is it not a blow also at freedom? It is interesting to note that these freedoms, embodied in the (American) Bill of Rights, were the result of denying that the "King can do no wrong." Is there not a greater menace to freedom in the belief that the "State can do no wrong?"
>
> I am not a Jehovah's Witness.

Crown Proceedings Bill. Under this new Bill in Britain, the King and the Crown will be brought on to the same legal footing as ordinary citizens. That means Government

Departments can be held responsible for their financial activities and be sued. Prior to this, the Departments had often been "graciously pleased" to allow a petition of right against themselves. Passage of the Bill also means that the Monarch can in future be sued. Note that similar legislation to this has been in force in Australia for several years. The King can do wrong, after all.

Divorce Court, Mr Justice Bonney. From today, the Court will require that **evidence of marital infidelity be provided in photographic form**. It was no longer acceptable that spying and raids into houses should be used. He indicated that he was wasting valuable Court time questioning witnesses to obtain facts that could be immediately established by a photograph.

Under the old regulations, two men would smash down a door, and act as witnesses and take notes. Under the new system, two men would smash down a door, and armed with a camera, would take photos. Fortunately, from the 1970's, a lot of doors were saved when Whitlam introduced his no-fault divorce legislation.

Comment. This small sample of rules and regulations is just the tip of the iceberg. Here they were, 18 months after the war ended, still forcing the population to do things that no one wanted to do. Slowly, as time passed and they were ever so slowly removed, resentment in the citizenry grew, until it got a chance to vote.

DON'T GIVE UP ON TRAVEL

It would be wrong, after the picture I have painted about the joys of travel, to think that all options were closed. Maybe you could move about some other way.

What about getting out your bike, and going to the shops on it. You could in those days park it outside and no one would pinch it. You could coast down the hills, being careful of the loose gravel, and tinkle on the bell, and feel the wind in your hair without a helmet. Think of what you would save on bus fare.

There are, however, a few problems. The bike has had no tyres since 1939, so the rubber has perished. There have been no new parts for all that time, so if anything has gone wrong mechanically, there are no replacements. Then the roads had deteriorated, so that the loose gravel is now widespread and deep. There are new restrictions that say you must have a light and a bell installed. Where can you buy a light in these austere days? Candles are not all that much use on a bike.

Perhaps a good Government Senator might help out. Well, here is what one had to say.

Ministry of Supply, Senator Ashley, Press release. Controls **over second-hand** passenger car tyres and all bicycle tyres have been lifted, the Minister for Supply, Senator Ashley, said yesterday. A published prediction that tyre rationing would end in three months was "guessing", he said. There would have to be an improvement in tyre production if rationing were to be lifted even in five months.

Because of the shortage of female labour and of cotton cord fabrics, it would be several weeks before bicycle tyres and tubes could be supplied freely. Manufacturers would ensure an equitable distribution in each State, and wholesalers would see that country and industrial areas were supplied on a fair basis.

Not much hope there. I suppose I have to admit that bikes are out. At least, for a few months.

Well, going back in time even further, **what about a horse?** They are making a comeback, especially in home deliveries. I admit they do come with problems, like getting the feed, and putting shoes on the beasts. Ten-year-old saddles are by now getting lumpy, and the bridles have all snapped. Perhaps they too are still out of the question.

But wait. There is a bit of a controversy in Sydney that might affect the situation. Let's have look at it.

> **Sydney City Council reports. An old concrete horse trough** in Pitt Street has emerged from its years-long obscurity to set the Lord Mayor, Alderman Bartley, one of his knottiest problems. The Australian Gaslight Company drew attention to the trough by complaining that it detracted from the brightness of its display windows.
>
> The Company suggested that it had more or less outlived its usefulness in that position, and should be removed. The Lord Mayor called for an investigation by the City Engineer, Mr Garnsey, who paid a visit to the trough, observed that there were few horses using it, and made a report to the Council. In the report, it was recommended that the trough be removed, and that some sort of drinking facility or fountain should replace it. The report did not satisfy a number of the aldermen who requested that a survey of horses should be taken along the route.
>
> So an inspector left the Town Hall to make an eight hour study of the horse trough. His notebook showed that 23 horses stopped between 8 a.m. and 5 p.m. The Council was now reasonably satisfied that the trough must stay, and was on the point of confirming this by resolution when Alderman Shannon, MLA, suggested

moving it to the other side of the street. He argued that the trough should be placed to be as readily accessible to weary horses returning home from the city late in the afternoon, rather than those going into the city in the morning.

So the Council agreed to move it to the opposite side of the street, provided the Gas Company paid the cost. The Town Clerk was on the point of writing to the Gas Company when a rescission motion was sent to him. These dissenters argued that the trough, on the other side of the street, would cause a traffic hazard. The Council resolved that the trough should remain where it is now, until further arguments relating to its positioning are considered.

That settles it. If horses can cause that much trouble, you don't want one. But there must be **some** solution. **I will keep thinking about it.**

PAGANISM IN AUSTRALIA

A Catholic priest was speaking at a Religion and Life Conference in Newcastle. He said that paganism was sweeping Australia, and it could only be remedied by big changes to the present godless education system. He saw examples of this in **the attention paid to jockeys, boxers, and professional footballers**. He also spoke out about the worship of the body, and the great deal of publicity given to the near nakedness shown in deliberately provocative swimming suits.

The only solution was a return to Christian values. This could not be done in the half hour per week allocated by public schools, and enough time should be provided for decent instruction. Furthermore, he said, Catholics were not getting a fair deal. They had to pay the same taxes as other people, and at the same time had to pay for their attendance at Catholic schools. "Why should they pay double taxation?" Relief should be provided through the taxation system.

Comment. What would he say about the attention paid today to our dazzling celebrity beauties and their boyfriends, divorces, fashion tips, and cats?

POST SCRIPT ON COUNTRY TRAIN TRAVEL

News item, Newcastle. A vast stampede occurred at Newcastle Station this morning, when 800 passengers attempted to board the Brisbane Mail on its way to Sydney. The Station Master was assaulted four times, and his trousers were torn in the fracas that developed.

There were no other trains scheduled to leave Newcastle today, and the holiday makers were determined not to be stranded. Although there were already 750 passengers on the train, the 800 somehow squeezed in. When the train stopped, the crowd rushed for the doors, and others clambered through the windows. Some children were then dragged through these windows, and stood in the aisle of the dogboxes.

The Station Master attempted to quell the crowd, and was "donged" on the head by an angry man. Later he was struck on the face, and trampled on. And that was when his trousers were badly ripped.

The train left with the hardy 1550 on board, standing cheek to jowl. It was reported that at Gosford, where there was normally a rush to the kiosk for refreshments, that not one person left the train, because they were frightened that they would not get back on it.

Comment. This was no one-off occurrence. It happened every weekend, and on all holidays, all over the nation.

APRIL NEWS ITEMS

Press report, April 1st. "Rumanian terrorists, trained by the British in 1940 in sabotage, last night blew up oil tanks in Haifa by using explosives. Twenty thousand tons of oil were still burning and damage will cost over one million Pounds"....

In case **anyone has the impression that terrorism is new**, I offer this piece. **Terrorism had already been around for many years,** and like now, affected civilians, and cities, and any vulnerable target. **No part of the world was immune**, though at the moment the Middle East was most often in the news.

Workers in the 21st Century expect to be paid for **not** working on Public Holidays. For example, if Anzac Day falls on a Wednesday, they expect to get a full day's pay. **But in 1947, this was not always the case....**

For example, **prior to now, coal miners lost a day's pay**. But from now on, they will be paid, but **only if they work the day before and the day after**. In a strike-prone industry, this measure was designed to at least get two working days out of them.

Queen Mary, on tour in South Africa, used her **umbrella to drive a native from the running board of her car** as she travelled through the Rand Mines. The native was shouting "I want to see my King" and he eventually **wrested the umbrella from the Queen**. Then he was arrested with a measure of violence.

You have four more days to **Find another Ball**.

Henry Ford died at the age of 83.

A student in Western Australia was surfing near Scarsborough. A garfish broke the water, and stuck its snout two inches into his face, near his eye. Locals said **he was the world's first speared fisherman**.

The Royal Easter Show at Sydney drew a record crowd of **200,376** on Good Friday....

But the Anglican Archbishop of Sydney said that the opening of the Show on Good Friday was a great indignity, and the ring **events to be held on Sunday were an affront to all Christians**....

The Show **was** to be **closed on the Sabbath**, but rain had forced the delay of many events, so a **make-up day on Sunday was held**. In a concession to the protesting Protestant Churches, **there was no entry fee on Sunday**.

The Chairman of the Sydney Milk Zone Dairymens' Committee (one of the regulatory Boards talked about earlier) **bemoaned** the fact that **13 per cent of the milk sent to Sydney was being used for cream**....

He explained that **Britain was crying out for milk, while we in Australia were luxuriating on cream**....

He appeared to forget that the nation had got no cream since 1940, because of our war efforts for Britain, and **now** that some regulations had been lifted, Australians were stuffing themselves. It turned out that **the orgy was short lived, and consumption soon dropped**.

It's official. Prime Minister Chifley advised Australians to **eat less so that the surplus could be sent to Britain**. Perhaps he too forgot that much food here was already severely rationed.

THESE ARE STRIKING TIMES

During the war, Trade Unions found it difficult to go out on strike. There were all sorts of Government laws and regulations that prevented them doing so. **But public opinion also imposed further restraints.** Who could be **so unpatriotic as to go on strike at a time of national emergency?** The nation needed every bit of production that could be mustered, it was popularly believed. So that striking was akin to sabotage.

During 1946, this sentiment began to change, with first the coal miners, and then the wharfies and transport workers downing tools and emptying their water bottles. And a host of minor Unions joined in sporadically as the year progressed. The problem was that, by 1947, everyone was fed up with all the restraints on labour and wages that the war had brought with it. Workers wanted a 40-hour week, and better working conditions. Coalminers wanted to come up to the surface and take a **shower**. Wharfies wanted to go to a place of work, and actually work, rather than take pot luck with the roster system. And of course, all of them wanted more wages.

Apart from the obvious disruption that the strikes caused to households, there was the added distress caused by their wildcat nature. No one had any idea **when** they might come.

Industrial report. One hundred shift-workers at the Government-controlled Mortlake gasworks decided yesterday morning to declare the gas strike on again. As a result, 300,000 premises joined to the Australian Gaslight Company's mains were without supplies last night. Rationing will be re-introduced to eke out supplies produced at the Manly and Oyster Bay works by staff volunteers.

On last Monday, a mass meeting of 2,000 gas workers decided against immediate strike action. Yesterday's decision took Union officials completely by surprise, and is reported to be unpopular with the majority of Union members. Trades Hall officials say the strike was a coup engineered by the Communist element in the Union.

By mid January, if the lady of the house in Sydney wanted to use gas to make a cup of tea or prepare an evening meal, then it was a gamble, and half the time she lost. If she wanted to have meat in this meal, she could not, because the butchers were out. If she wanted to go shopping by tram or bus, then expect a long wait or a long walk; good luck in getting home. If she was lucky enough to be getting something from overseas, then there was no point in holding her breath. The wharfies too were on strike. If she wanted to use electricity for meals or lighting in the evening, then she would surely get some. But when, and for how long, was a secret that was well kept.

Needless to say, all this activity – or really, inactivity – hurt the housewives and their families. The Letters pages to the newspapers were full of protests, and much analysis of the situation, some of it sensible, was forthcoming. A typical very annoying strike was the meat strike in January. Here the real problem was that Government had **fixed the prices that consumers would pay**. On the other hand, wholesalers were caught with a drought and a desire to make more money, so **they** raised their prices. This left the butcher in the street with ever-decreasing margins. So most of them closed their shops. Sydney butchers, after haggling for a week or two, went back to work, with a bit more money from higher retail prices. But not Newcastle. There the butchers hung out for another futile month.

Letters, D Corfe. Officials of the ACTU, the Gas Employees' Union, the tramway employees, and the retail butchers **all say that in striking they are only claiming justice.** But by their very actions, that justice which they claim for themselves, they deny to others.

Can these men tell what wrong the housewives, children, and men in other industries have done to the Unions that the innocent should be made to suffer by being without gas, meat, or transport, and wherein lies their responsibility? Was it because they exercised their voting rights and placed in power a party pledged to uphold the principle of arbitration that they must now be punished by the Unions?

I appeal to the Prime Minister, the Premier, and the leaders of the ACTU to inform us, the victims of the strikes, what we are to do to secure for ourselves the queer thing that they call justice, which the dictionary defines as "fairness in dealing with others".

Letters, G de Lissa. The most potent factor activating our industrial unrest is the uncontrolled falling off in the workers' standard of living. When the prices of commodities rise, the obvious need is for more money which, if attained, merely stimulates the vicious circle of higher prices. Reduction or removal of taxation will not relieve the situation because it does not sufficiently benefit the low wage earner.

The solution lies in lowering the cost of commodities, and this can be accomplished by **government control of primary industry, together with rigid price control of primary products**. To reduce by these means the cost of all primary production to pre-war (or earlier) levels will reverse the direction of the vicious circle, and quickly start the restoration of our seriously devalued currency.

The type of credit developed to win the war can be re-developed to win the peace. Repayment would come concurrently with the unwinding of the circle, and the consequent release of currency for revenue without detriment to living standards.

Meat and Allied Industry Federation, Mr Herbert, Secretary, said yesterday that most butchers' shops in Sydney and Newcastle will be closed from today because of their inability to operate within the law. It was specifically a protest against the current price-fixing system.

He said that **"we don't think of it as a strike but as a cessation of business**. At present, butchers are unable to get supplies at prices which enable them to work within the law, and therefore, standing down of employees will be justified."

Mr Herbert described reports of Canberra officials that the closure would last only a few days as "wishful thinking." He added that "we don't know how long the shops will remain closed, but this time we have to stand firm if any reforms are to be introduced. Our butcher complaint is not against the producers, but against the principle that one side of the trade is controlled, and not the other."

The chairman of the Carcase Butchers' Association said last night that stock coming forward for slaughter was only a quarter of normal requirements, and there was little in cold store.

Commonwealth Price Commissioner. Mr E McCarthy in Canberra stated that **400 meat retailers were listed for**

prosecution for charging excess prices to customers. This was a continuation of the decisive action he had been taking against wholesale butchers for months. It was noted that meat yesterday was **sold in only about 50 of the 1250 retail butchers shops in Sydney**.

These two items are indicative of the sideshow in Newcastle.

Newcastle, Mayoral announcement.   Alderman Quinlan said today that large quantities of meat were finding their way into Newcastle through illegal channels. Municipal **regulations** demand that all meat brought into the district for public consumption should be accompanied by a certificate issued by the slaughteryards that the meat is fit to eat.

It is well known that inter-city expresses reaching Newcastle from Sydney during the local butchers' strike are known as "beef specials", because **almost all passengers have chilled steaks or roasts secreted in their baggage**. Trains and cars arriving from Sydney and other centres where meat is now sold are met by hundreds of householders anxious to take delivery of orders entrusted to friendly travellers and relatives.

Councillor Quinlan said that "we are not taking sides in the strike. The only consideration is the health and welfare of the people. We are not concerned about meat brought in for consumption by the individual or his relatives."

The Secretary of Newcastle Trades Hall said today that the Prime Minister, Mr Chifley, will on Monday discuss the strike position with a deputation appointed at a public meeting at Newcastle on Monday night.

Newcastle news item: Yesterday morning Mr E. Wellings, owner of a Newcastle hamburger shop, had plenty of coupons, but no meat. Mr Wellings has not been able to buy meat, because of the butcher's strike. He was told he could bring meat into Newcastle if he submitted it for inspection to the Newcastle Abattoirs. He was also told he could buy meat in Booral, a village not far from country Dungog.

He drove 54 miles to Booral and bought 80 pounds of meat – joints for his neighbours and steak for his shop. He surrendered his own and his neighbours' coupons. He drove back to Newcastle and took his meat to the Abattoirs.

There it was confiscated because slaughtering at Booral had been **supervised by a police sergeant and not supervised by a certified meat inspector**, as the Newcastle Abbatoirs Act requires. Mr Wellings asked permission to take the meat back to Booral and regain the coupons he had surrendered. This was refused. Mr Wellings intends to appeal various decisions.

The meat industry was not the only one on strike.

Funeral Directors Association, Press statement. There appeared to be no hope that striking Sydney gravediggers would return to work before next Thursday, at the earliest. By that time, about 280 bodies in funeral parlours would be waiting to be buried. Mr L. Mammish said that the mass-meeting of diggers, to be held today, would be futile, because they would recommend a return to work only if certain conditions were met. But those conditions were impossible. He went on to say the Union wanted to play with a two-headed penny. If the Court gives them some better clauses in their awards, they take them, but if there were other clauses they do not like, they go on strike.

Only one funeral was held at Rookwood cemetery yesterday. The son of the deceased, and a friend who was a funeral director, dug the grave themselves in the family plot. The Undertakers Union said last night that where funerals were conducted before the end of the strike, those graveyards would be declared "black".

The reaction to the various strikes at the national level was to run for cover. The Leader of the Opposition, Mr Menzies, was outspoken about Labor's inaction.

I am delighted that the Prime Minister is even **talking** about action in relation to industrial troubles. I cannot remember any single instance in any industrial dispute at any time during his Prime Ministership about which he has **done** anything at all.

With skilful publicity he appears to have built a reputation as a strong man by doing exactly nothing. Action is certainly necessary. Even the amazing patience of the Australian people must be wearing a little thin by now.

The Leader of the Country Party, Mr Fadden. If the widespread industrial unrest is at long last tiring the Prime Minister, then he has only himself to blame. The Australian people, particularly the housewives, tired of repeated strikes years ago.

During the elections, **Mr Chifley** championed the right to strike. **He said it was a fundamental right of men to leave work if they were dissatisfied.** The Prime Minister's advocacy of the right to strike has boomeranged on him. He is now, very belatedly, attempting to get out of the trouble he has brought on himself. Had the Government early in office taken action, Australia would now be free from the industrial turmoil it has experienced.

> We will await with interest positive evidence of the results of this new policy of direct action, instead of speeches, in the settlement of industrial disputes.

It is interesting to note that whatever action was taken to limit strikes, and whatever action was not taken, they went on with no signs of decreasing for decades. This includes the 16 years that Menzies was in power, starting from 1950, and beyond.

The 40-hour week. Round about now, discussions about reducing the length of the working week in NSW got serious. Before that, there was some wild talk from Mr McGirr, the Premier, to pass various forms of a bill to cut the working week to forty hours. This would have meant that most employees could look forward to an extra four to eight hours of leisure-time each week.

The suggested reforms raised howls of protest. The arguments against it were many and varied, but they all came down to the claim that if everyone worked fewer hours, the prices of everything would rise. And of course, employers opposed it because its introduction would raise their costs. Another interested party was the Federal Government, which was talking about introducing a similar clause into its awards. In all, there was a period of intense manoeuvring, and lots of strikes, but from about now, the 40-hour week was introduced in the various States for all employees on State awards, and then flowed through into private enterprise. The bush-lawyers came out firing:

> **A problem is** the determination by some Unions that 40-hours means that the work will be done in **five equal shifts of eight hours**. Many employers say that this is not specified in the Act, and they say it means

that the employees can be used in big or little lots as they want to use them.

This last provision was a worry to workers. **If** it were implemented as suggested here, workers could be rostered **to work at any time at all, in shifts of any length, provided the weekly total did not exceed forty hours**. Obviously, this was not the intent of the legislation. So, within a day:

Sydney railwaymen decided to take drastic action to enforce strict observation of the 40-hour week. They decided that they would not work overtime until working rosters were altered to conform to their demands. Other unions are expected to take similar action.

There were others muddying the situation. A number of engine drivers indicated that they would enforce a closed shop, and that would prevent new drivers from joining their ranks. This meant that they would get more overtime. At the same time, the Commissioner for Railways said it was not possible, with an industry that worked round the clock, to have shifts end at some pre-determined time. "Should an engine driver leave his train when his eight-hour shift is up? What about an airline pilot in mid-air?" One alarmist **Letter-writer** suggested that the new law meant that teachers would have to spend forty hours actually in the classroom.

The solution to all this was to recognise that there was no **one** solution. There were a number of different situations, and each of them required **an industry solution**. The McGirr Government was at fault here because it did not do enough to make this apparent when it introduced the legislation. For example, the coal miners found the new deal attractive, because they had previously worked five day-time shifts a week, and also Saturday mornings. Now they simply dropped Saturday work. Others, such as railway workers and power generation workers, were in a more complicated position. They had gone from elation at the time the new law was announced, to a bit of glee when they thought of the extra overtime, to great alarm when the prospect of working lots of broken shifts was suggested.

It only took a few months of the usual strikes before settlements were reached, even in the most troubled industries, as gradually industry-by-industry solutions were worked out.

STRIKE PAY

When workers followed their Union leaders and went on strike, they of course were not paid by their bosses. If the strike appeared to be a long one, say for two weeks or more, the Union usually gave the workers a small sum each week, and this was called "strike-pay". It wasn't nearly as much as their normal pay, but it kept body and soul together for a few more weeks.

These payments were essential for any strike to succeed. A few years from now, in the coal miners' strike in NSW **in 1949, Chifley famously froze Union funds**, so that strike -pay stopped and the strike broke within a day.

Thousands of workers and Unionists swore then that they would never again vote for Chifley, and they stuck to that at the next election. This is one reason that Chifley was tossed out at that time.

MAY NEWS ITEMS

Immigration Minister, **Arthur Calwell**, has a difficult decision to make. 400,000 Maltese citizens are anxiously waiting for his approval for them to migrate to Australia. Their problem is that they are of Mediterranean origin, and **are of a swarthy colour**. Indeed, under some definitions, **they might be described as coloured**....

But **Australia has a White Australia Policy**, and our good friend Calwell determined that Australia would stay as white as snow. No matter, he says, that the Maltese are only skin-deep darkish, and no matter that **they are citizens of the British Empire. Australia must stay white**, he says....

This was the beginning of a period of years where Calwell did everything in his power to **save us from the migrating Asian hordes, and keep our blood exceptionally pure**.

During the war, all petrol companies pooled their resources and delivered petrol to garages in trucks that carried **no branding**. They poured the **rationed** fuel into their own pits at the garages, and sold it under their own brand at garages that had as many as **a dozen different-branded bowsers.....**

This system was about to end. Competition was branding to be allowed at all stages, and this applied to the garages as well. So it was **the beginning of the end for garages carrying multiple brands**. Within a decade, these were disappearing, and being replaced by those carrying a single brand. At this time also, **garages were promoted from "garages" to "service stations"**.

There was some bated breath in the NSW town of Berry yesterday. **Two bulls** were being driven down the main street to markets when they suddenly veered into a shop. This was not just an ordinary shop. **It was a china shop.** They meandered down one long aisle, sniffing and wheezing. Round the corner, ever so sedately, and up the second aisle, **still poking their runny noses into things of interest**....

They stood for a full minute in the doorway, deciding whether to buy, and then heeded the man with the stockwhip, and went to meet their new owners....

At this stage, there were no bulls in the china shop.

NSW and Queensland will hold State elections on the coming Saturday. Since **pubs are closed for the day** on these auspicious occasions, **no grog will flow in either State**. Serious drinkers **near the common border** of the two States will be denied the pleasure of border hopping to save their lives. This is a matter for much vocal concern.

Question time. Who was the better singer? We all know that it came down to two greats, **Bing or Frank.** **But who do you think was the absolute best?** It's *White Christmas* and *Lazybones* versus *Saturday Night* and *Dream.*

And, now one for the ladies. What did you do with your bobby-sox? Not thrown out, **surely**.

ANOTHER PIECE ON TRAVEL.

Commercial air travel was negligible, so that most people entered and left the nation by **ship**. Since most of the major liners had been sequestered by government early in the war, there was a huge back-log of shipping. And most of the berths available went to official categories, of one sort or another. The two Letters below illustrate the case for an unfortunate English lady.

Letters, DISGUSTED ENGLISHWOMAN. I challenge the statement that only 130 berths were allocated to passengers to Britain last month. During April, the *Rimutaka, Javanese Prince, Sarpendon*, and *Wairang*i, not to mention passenger-carrying cargo ships, have left for England.

These figures seem hard to reconcile. Perhaps the Ministry of British Shipping would tell me why I, a British woman, **stranded here by the war**, and anxious to return to England for permanent residence, am unable to get a passage, and yet numerous Australians are granted passage because they want to try and get a job in England, or chase up some man, something equally frivolous.

Reply from British Ministry of Supply. A British lady, "Disgusted Englishwoman" refers to a shortage of shipping berths to the UK, and asserts that numerous Australians are granted passage for "frivolous reasons."

Might I remind her that the **Passenger Priority Committee** carefully considers all applications, and berths are not allocated for frivolous reasons. It is appreciated that the inability to secure a berth is, to say the least, annoying to the party concerned, but this is primarily due to the large number of passenger steamers lost during the war. The number left is insufficient for the great number of persons requiring transport, which includes released Prisoners of war and internees, Service dependents, Merchant Navy personnel, etc.

The actual number of berths allocated to non-Government civilians during April was 134. The writer mentions the *Rimutaka* carrying 300 passengers. This is correct, but part of her accommodation was used for New Zealand, and part was required by Army, Navy, and Government authorities for service dependents etc. The number of non-government civilians was less than 300.

Plane travel. Plane travel for the nervous passenger was a bit more worrying than now. By the end of the war, the monoplanes and bi-planes that Smithy used to buzz round in were mainly gone for commercial purposes, and they had been replaced by 30-seaters with two engines.

Then again, much air travel was by seaplane. The Catalina had been used a lot in WWII by our Air Force, and now these planes were being converted to commercial travel. Some people felt uneasy during take-offs and landings. But they did carry a lot of traffic.

Writers had`their say.

Letters, Gerry Crooks. I want to travel overseas, but I can't get a booking on a ship, and so I have been looking at plane travel. Let me sum up a month's research on the subject. The trip is too pricey. The fare would take up one full year of my wages. I would have to book months in advance, and then I might not get on that flight if some bigwig came and took my seat at the last moment. There are only a few flights per week, and these are uncertain about time of arrival and departure. No one knows how long it will take, except to say that it will take longer than scheduled. I want to go to a wedding in London, but it seems it will be over before I get there. And there is apparently no good cheap transport from the airport to where I want to go. I will stay at home and sulk.

Of course, the aircraft industry was just in its infancy, as far as shifting a large number of passengers was concerned. Many of the problems and opportunities for plane travel are covered in the following article.

Aviation Correspondents, Canberra. Passengers across the globe can now readily board an aeroplane and fly to almost anywhere. At least in theory. There are a couple of drawbacks. Firstly, many places are not covered by flights. And secondly, **the price is too high** for the average man to afford.

Prices to London are 375 Pounds, to USA they are 300 Pounds, and to NZ they are 30 Pounds. (Note that the average Australian annual income was 600 Pounds). Of course, this is not a problem for the fortunate few who travel on Government business, but for the average man, one of "the masses", it is too much. He will have to wait till shipping services get back to normal before he can go overseas.

It is hard to fathom why air services are so expensive, if you just do arithmetic. There are many contradictions in pricing, but it is clear that airlines will charge what they will get away with. They call it supply and demand balancing. It is good to see then that the supply looks like picking up.

For example, Tasman Empire Airways have recently introduced **double-decker flying-boats** on the Sydney to Auckland service. The new boats carry twice the number as before, and carry more freight, but the price remains the same.

There is an explanation of the high price to London. Qantas is using the modified bomber planes, the Lancasters, because no other type of plane is available at the moment. **The Lancasters carry only six passengers**, yet the servicing costs would be about the same as the Skymasters, which carry 33 passengers on overseas flights. Later this year, Qantas expects to have 44-passenger Constellations for the UK route, and Mr Hudson Fysh expects the price to fall by about 100 Pounds. Most analysts say that this price is still too high, and he will operate with small loads. It is a long way from filling planes with six passengers to carrying forty four.

Still, overall, competition is increasing, and so too is the availability of shipping. If the prices do then come down, and **the masses do take more to air travel for pleasure instead of business**, it is possible that the industry could do better than just survive.

Let me point out though, that Lockheed was now on the job, and its Constellation was soon to be available on quite a few routes. Other sleek, large planes were about to appear. Some of the Australian airlines would be able to buy a few of those planes in the near future, and you could say, a new industry, for the transportation of the masses, was born.

NSW LATE-CLOSING REFERENDUM

Throughout the war, conditions in hotels right round Australia deteriorated. In fact, before the war, they were pretty bad, with scungy bars, stand-as-you-drink facilities, and redback spiders under the dunny seats. Now, in 1947, all of these old vices were still there, but added to that was a severe beer shortage. This meant that pubs were forever running out of beer, and wine and spirits so that, about eighty percent of the time, the pubs stood empty of customers. In the other twenty percent, when the beer was "on", patrons rushed to the bars, and fought their way through a crowd of drinkers, and got their middies so that they could stand cheek to jowl with other men, trying to drink enough beer in a short time to keep them going till the next time.

Because the beer was usually "on" in the late afternoon, after work finished, this charming scene – repeated three times a week if you were lucky – was known as the "six o'clock swill." As an aside, I mention that pigs persistently wrote to the papers complaining that pigs as a species were being defamed by such a comparison.

One reason for the shortage of beer was that hundreds of thousands of men discharged from the military services had been flooding back into the country with their tongues hanging out. Another was that war-time shortages of available grain for beer-making were still with the nation. And much of that grain was still being sent overseas to stop people in Europe starving to death. The breweries too played their part. They were in a quite comfortable position, where every drop of beer they produced was sold the minute they offered it, and it was sold through hotels that were – at that time – mainly owned by the breweries themselves. The brewers were in no desperate hurry to rock the boat, given that major reforms might involve them in expensive upgrades to premises.

This situation was made worse by the absence of alcoholic alternatives. Virtually the only **wine** for sale in Australia was fortified, with port, sherry, and muscat, in a brown paper bag, as the favourites. Table wines, such as chardonnay and shiraz, were a bit too sophisticated for this nation of beer guzzlers. Also, spirits, like whiskey and brandy, were imported from overseas, and so were impossible to get. There was a company in Victoria that, about this time, started to produce an Australian whiskey under the name of CORIO. Unfortunately, there was also a refinery, Commonwealth Oil Refineries, that produced an oil that was sold under the brand of COR 10. The similarity in name, and - some say - in product, had an unfortunate marketing effect on the whiskey company's sales, and it had a lot of problems from that time on.

So, in NSW, now this all came to a head. For a year, the Government had been under pressure to change liquor laws. Soldiers overseas, for example in Britain, had seen more civilised drinking, and wanted it here. Gradually pressure mounted to the stage where a referendum was held to determine whether the pubs should continue to close at 6 pm, or whether they should stay open till 10 o'clock. Of course, any such change would not make much difference to the chaotic situation that drinkers now faced, but it tackled the problem of real thirsts right now, and would presumably lead to better changes in the future.

Forces against ten o'clock closing. Not everyone thought that the extension of pub trading hours was a good idea. Among the churches, there were a few who looked at a wider perspective than the simple matter of closing hours.

> **Reverend W C Goughlan,** of the Church of England Social Order Movement, said that the worst feature of this referendum is that it isolates a single element – the closing hour – and confines the recording of public opinion to that one issue. In consequence,

the peoples' attention is distracted from the really important ingredients of the problem of drinking and drunkenness, such as the psychological conditioned and environmental pressures which drive so many people to drink overmuch. Whichever way the vote goes, the community will still have on its hands those deeper and knottier problems, the solution of which will demand a comprehensive and long-range programme touching every department of corporate living.

Other Church correspondents were less inclined to wisdom, and were more combative. In the opinion of the Council of Churches, through Rev A E Eastman, "the Churches had spoken with one voice in calling for **the retention of six o'clock closing**. We have absolute confidence in the hope of a majority, which in its incidence will, to a great degree, make the proposed iniquitous Liquor Act innocuous. It will be Democracy's answer to the liquor magnates who seek profits to the detriment of the social, moral, and spiritual welfare of the State."

Paddington Youth Christian Club, a Church spin-off, puts a different slant on it. Mr Gledhill, Superintendent, said "here in Paddington, there are 20 hotels and a number of wine bars in an area about a mile square. Many of these are close to dance halls, picture theatres, and other places of amusement. What is going to happen to the youth in the area if late trading is allowed? The problem of juvenile delinquency is bad enough now. Are we going to accentuate it by encouraging parents to go to the 'luxury lounge' while leaving their children to go to the devil? Under 6 o'clock closing, many young people have not acquired the drink habit, but with bars open at night, temptation will be put in their way compared with which 'pig-trough' drinking will be a minor evil indeed."

Then we have Letters that take a very different tack. These two look at overseas drinking.

> **Letters, Glynn Foster**. There will be thousands of deluded voters favouring 10 o'clock closing, because we have been told so much about Continental conditions and 'civilised drinking' conditions, and certainties of less drunkenness. If it were certain that later hours would bring with it less drunkenness, none would oppose it. However, those soldiers who have been used to American and European beer, which is weaker than ours, have shown beyond doubt that **they cannot handle our strong stuff**. If we are to have Continental hours and Continental lounges, then let us **have a similar alcoholic content**, and parallel Continental conditions

On the other hand, Isabel Tyso really likes the idea of late closing.

> As an inhabitant of Tasmania, where late closing is in force, I am well acquainted with 10 o'clock closing. Often after dinner, we stroll along some lovely paths, and at the end of the walk, we call in at a pub for a 'pick-me-up'. It is so pleasant to be able to sit in the cool, and sip a glass of cider. Why should not the rest of Australia wake up, and enjoy life as we do in Tasmania. We do not hurry, and we get there just the same. I think the closing hour of 6 o'clock is not only arbitrary, but absurd. Why subject yourself to such tyranny?

But there is another view of the idyllic life in Tassie. Rev Touchwell tells us that "there is no question that 10 o'clock closing increases enormously the amount of drinking. It is the young people who crowd into the hotel lounges in the evening with appalling results. We have an appalling number of road accidents due to drink, and drunken minors are everywhere."

There were other objections. "Where there is 10 o'clock closing – Queensland and Tasmania – there is still a six o'clock rush, **and** a ten o'clock rush. Drunkenness in Queensland has increased 36 per cent since drinking hours were increased. Where there is "leisure" evening drinking, there is increased drunkenness; it is sapping Britain's strength, it is ten times more evident in America than in prohibition days, it is seven times worse in France than here."

So these arguments for early closing went on. Some of them were true, lots of them were false. And on the other side were similar claims for the benefits of late closing. Here, it was said, the choice is between enlightened drinking conditions and the present chaotic trading hours. Further, it was argued that, under the present system, drinking was compressed into an hour-and-a-half. Under the proposed regime, workers would eat at home, before taking a drink. And with their wives too, in decent comfortable conditions. And of course, there were references to France. "In France, drunkenness is almost unknown, and is considered a social disgrace."

One loud argument against change was the claim that it was the breweries that would benefit from new hours. Letter after Letter talked about "fat brewers stuffing their pockets with their ill gotten gains." This prompted a gentleman called Tom Watson to place a large advertisement in the Sydney papers. **Watson was the long-standing General**

Manager for Tooth's Breweries, a position he held for donkey's years. He, in noble terms, pointed out the great concern that the breweries had for drinkers, and how 10 o'clock closing would soon make everything rosy again.

He got a lot of response, including the one below.

Letters, A Serious Drinker. When this letter was published on February 4, I was one of a number of serious drinkers who wanted a beer every afternoon after work. There were no clubs in our provincial city yet, so we met up in a grand old pub. We were considerably outraged by Tom Watson's letter, and vowed that we would give up drinking Tooth's beer as a protest. Not to-day of course, but at some time in the future, quite soon.

He got us angry for a number of reasons. He had been in charge of Tooth's for as long as any of us could remember, since the early 1930's. And he had earned the reputation of being a complete autocrat, an enemy of any form of unionisation, and – so we then thought, from hundreds of miles away – cold and heartless with no regard for his employees, and certainly none for his drinkers. To have him come out, on the eve of a referendum on ten o'clock closing, and give us a mealy mouthed apologia for poor beer supplies, was about as bad as he could get.

On top of that, he blamed shortages of beer on shortages of all the components that went into the finished product. We argued that this was his problem, not ours. He was paid to get the ingredients and make beer with them, and deliver the beer to us, and then we would do our bit, and drink it. Then there were his references to the landlords, almost sanctifying them. They were, in fact, not at all sacred. (**Comment.** Actually, at the time, landlords were pretty rough, and many of them were outright scoundrels. The vision of them doling out bottled beer in a careful and considerate manner to devoted customers was rubbish. A better picture would be of two dozen men, full as bulls, drinking after-hours behind locked doors, with the local police sergeant, and paying inflated prices to this benevolent host.)

Then there was the creature comfort in pubs. For an hour each day, we stood, shoulder to shoulder, in a crowd of 100 rowdy and sometimes pugilistic men, and gulped as much beer as we could buy. That was when the beer was "on". About three afternoons a week, when it was "off", we went home dry. There was no hope of bottled beer for the plebs; and the only wine you could buy was port, sherry, and brown muscat. For the ladies, there was always a palatial parlour, where half a dozen of them could sit and shell their peas, with their hair up in rollers.

Watson's promise that things would soon get better, "in a month or two", did not impress us at all. (**Comment**. And in fact, it took about twenty years for things to change much.) The trouble was, for us, that despite our unremitting antagonism to Watson, we too wanted ten o'clock closing to be passed at the referendum. So we had to vote as he advocated. But not because of that letter. **That** only hardened our dislike of him. And I am sure that it was the hypocrisy of this letter that turned the tide against 10 o'clock closing.

This letter was written by Fred Mays, aged 85, who says he is still about to give up on Tooth's beer, at some time, **soon.**

The propaganda war. Both sides in this campaign were in full battle mode from as early as November 1946. For three and a half months, they hit the newspapers and the air waves and the man-in-the-street with a constant barrage of just why they should vote this way or that.

It really did not matter much if the statements they made were right or not. Everyone knew that. After all, for example, the breweries and hoteliers were after increased profits. On the other hand, churches and temperance groups wanted people to drink less or nothing. And so, as is inevitable in this type of dispute, both sides avoided expressing their real aims, and instead talked about increased or decreased comfort, or about women coming or not coming out for a drink at night, and about whether the poor worker could or could not get the beer he wanted. In fact, he could not; and did not for years after 1947. Because, a point ignored by all in this controversy, there was nothing in this referendum that would increase the supply of beer one little bit.

The newspaper ads were big and highly emotive. Some of them were a half-page in the *Sydney Morning Herald*, a rarity in those austere days. Often, near the polling day, there were ten such ads in a day. For the average reader, if they noticed them at all by that stage, it was just to see who was sponsoring the ad this time.

The referendum results. The early results on Saturday night showed an emphatic win for 6 o'clock closing. Of the almost one and a half million votes counted, 925,000 were for early closing, and 520,000 were for late, giving the former group a majority of about 400,000. This resounding victory **emboldened a few groups to demand further changes immediately**. The Temperance Alliance called for strict enforcement of the laws on hotel **accommodation**, which was an issue hardly raised in the campaign. Then they went on to agitate for the "Local Option", by which the voters in the upcoming election would vote whether **their electorate** should become "wet or dry". A more sober statement was issued by the liquor trade representatives, who said that hotel conditions would be improved, **but not immediately**. In fact, as it turned out, they did keep the latter part of that promise.

The *SMH* editorial argued that the people of NSW had simply registered an obvious protest vote. They had seen that the whole referendum was aimed at improving the profits of the brewers, and offered no extra beer or extra services. The voters had registered their "disgust at present drinking conditions… and that extending hours would simply extend the abuses" which now prevailed.

So, for the winners, this was a moment of glee. The baddies had lost. But on reflection, and on looking back, it was a very brief moment. Because, with the victory, nothing had changed. The next Monday, the six o'clock swill was still there, perhaps, if you were lucky. There was still little beer and no seats in hotels, the ladies were still in the parlour, there was a chance of getting a punch in the head if you weren't careful in the crowd.

In short, conditions were still terrible. And they stayed that way until 1954 when another referendum was a bit more successful. In the meantime, there was a brief period when the pubs were closed between six-thirty and seven-thirty, but that satisfied no one. These steps towards civilised drinking were quite small really, but they were in the right direction. Certainly things by then were better than the 1947 swill.

REMEMBER EMPIRE DAY.

May 24th each year was celebrated for two reasons. The first was for the rather mundane rejoicing that the British Empire round the world did, in order to express its joy that God had so blessed the British peoples. Here, in Australia, it took the form of austere public ceremonies in Town Hall, speeches at school assemblies, and editorials in the major papers. There was nothing to stir the masses there.

In the evening, things changed, because Empire Day turned into Cracker Night, and the nation was lit up from one end to the other with bonfires. Big, beautiful bonfires, fueled by second-hand tyres, and by the inevitable palings off the fences of those who weren't there. Then there were the crackers, little Tom Thumbs, right through to the Double Bungers, that always seemed to get into letter-boxes. Or a few were tied to dogs' tails. Sparklers for the timid, rockets for the adventurous. A great night that unfortunately has gone away. Every year, there was a handful of people who had parts of their body, or their eyesight, blown away in all the explosions, so gradually the authorities imposed enough restrictions to kill Cracker Night. What a pity.

REMEMBER BOXING

Boxing was part and parcel of the Australian way of life, especially for men. Every week, some major bout was fought in the nation's stadiums, generally to full houses, amid a lot of excitement. Betting on the outcome was illegal. And that, of course, added to its appeal both at the stadium and across the countryside. (Just for fun, ask some old-timer if he remembers the Tommy Burns versus Vic Patrick fight).

JUNE NEWS ITEMS

The Viceroy of India, Lord Mountbatten, is about to sign off on **the Independence of India** from Britain. There are currently fears that various disputes arising, especially **between Hindus and Muslims**, will mean strife in the future. In fact, many years of bloodshed and tears passed **before stability between India and the newly-formed Pakistan was reached**.

Mankind is always ready to accept **the benefits of advancing technology**. This is again apparent from the speed with which **letter-bombs** are being adopted by **terrorists in Europe**. These new and innocent-looking little packages, each containing some ground gelignite and a detonator, are turning up in Britain, and **blowing the hands off the lucky recipients....**

They are becoming popular world-wide. The latest batch in Britain **was posted in Italy**.

In London, a married soldier was accused of **murdering his wife in a much publicised trial. His defence was that she nagged him non-stop.** Overwhelming evidence was presented that she was **an inveterate nagger**, and that **he** had not if fact been in any way delinquent. She also manipulated him constantly. For example, she pretended to have meningitis when he was about to make a career move, and lost him his promotion....

The soldier was found not guilty of murder, but **guilty of manslaughter.** The gallery **burst into applause** when the verdict was handed down.

Housewives and fishermen have long been confused by **the different names given to various types of fish**. The **Commonwealth Fisheries** has now stepped in, and said this malfeasance must stop....

In future, the **official name** for blackfish will be luderick, and yellow bellies will become **callops**, and jewfish will be called calloways. Perch will be known as bass, and kingfish will be called yellowtail kingfish....

A month later, the *SMH* published **a series of Letters** from fishermen, professionals and amateur, claiming that **catches of all these fish had diminished drastically** since these names were made official, and calling for the situation to be reversed.

A month **after the Japanese Emperor was stripped of his divinity**, he made a public appearance in Osaka. He was surrounded by a screaming crowd of **over a million persons, all shouting banzais in his honour**. "The demonstrations by all classes show how much **the Emperor is respected right across the nation**".

The reason for **Queensland's static sheep population**, by contrast with the rest of Australia, has been shown to be because of the **very high level of fluorine in bore water**. The sheep are developing fluorosis, that **reduces fertility**. It can have the same effect of humans, but the water can be treated to remove this....

Comment. Over the years, it has been suspected that **Queensland's notorious resistance to fluoridation** of town water is related to the fear of fluorosis from bore water.

CHARLES COUSENS

Early years. Charles Cousens was a military man from birth. He was born at legendary Poona in India, son of an artillery officer of very pukka breed, in 1903. He was educated in military schools, firstly at Wellington College in Berkshire, and later at Sandhurst Military College, for training army officers. He was commissioned, and posted to – you guessed it – the North West Frontier in India in 1924. He was over six feet tall, good looking in the Errol Flynn mould, good at sport, and gregarious though reserved by nature. He resigned from the Army in 1927, and worked his way to Australia. Here, by the start of the war, he was working as a radio announcer with 2GB, he had a large following, and a smooth voice that won him many female admirers.

When war came, he enlisted as a Captain, and was posted to Malaya. He was with the 2nd/19th Battalion when Singapore fell in February, 1942, and he was imprisoned briefly in Changi. When the Japanese found out he was a radio announcer, he was removed from there and ended up in Tokyo in July. He remained there for most of the time until the end of the war in later 1945.

Later years. From 1942 to 1945, Cousens was required by the Japanese to help them produce various radio propaganda programmes that were transmitted to Australian and American servicemen throughout the Pacific. The idea of these was, one way or another, to damage their morale, and make them unwilling to fight. For example, the Japanese constantly bragged about their military victories, real and imagined. They talked about how nice it would be to be at home with their girlfriends, and asked whether those girl friends were being faithful. They talked about mum's home cooking, and little brothers, and any nostalgic pet dog they could dream up.

Cousens throughout his years in Japan, and subsequently in law courts at home, was quite adamant that he performed these tasks under constant threat of punishment or death. He maintained that at every new step, he resisted until he was actually struck or was promised torture or death if he did not comply. Thereafter, he complied, but in such a way that he at least took the mickey out of the programme, or slyly destroyed their credibility, and even at times sent off information that was of strategic value to our military forces.

Back in Australia, it was claimed that he had **not** been coerced, at least not all the time. It was noted that he lived for a long time in Tokyo's second best hotel, and that he wore civilian clothes a lot. He was photographed at a party with Japanese nationals from his radio station – and from that it was suggested that he led a high life. It was also argued that at night he would at times go back to the radio station, and talk freely with the other announcers, and this was seen as not the behaviour of a typical prisoner of war. He also had a room of his own, hot and cold running water, and good food.

Throughout the war, his broadcasts were heard right across the Pacific, and in Australia on short-wave radio. One particular programme that he produced, *Zero Hour*, became famous with Australian and US servicemen because it was a subtle piece of Japanese propaganda that kept the troops up with the latest pop music and was especially noted because his announcer for this show was a girl who became known as Tokyo Rose. This lass had been born in Hawaii, and was in Japan at the start of hostilities. Because of her good grasp of English, she was directed to broadcast for Cousens' unit. Unfortunately, her husky tones earned her quite a name, and at the end of the war she was tried in America and found guilty of treason.

Cousens' broadcasts to the troops apparently met with a mixed reception, and this carried over into the emotions of the nation when he **was later tried in Australia**. There were some who were satisfied that he did his best to undermine the propaganda. For example, he then always spoke in a flat dull tone, not at all like the expressive voice that he used at home. He called every typist-error exactly as it was, with an injection of ridicule. At the end of violent messages of military triumph, he would play a tune that suggested that it may be rubbish. For example, he played a well known *Tell it to the Marines* on one occasion, and *Abdull the Bull Bull* on another. There can be no doubt that manipulating messages like this was a dangerous occupation.

The trouble for Cousens was that not every one picked up his subtleties. Irregular listeners were less likely, poor reception took its toll. Undoubtedly some of the messages were more obscure than subtle. But one group saw no merit in them at all, and this was the Official Listening Post back in Australia which recorded a great deal of his programmes, and produced them with malice in his subsequent trial. Another disapproving listener was Douglas McArthur, who also took a strong dislike to Tokyo Rose.

At the end of the war, Cousens was shipped home to Australia and; while under open arrest, was charged under Section 40 of the Army Act: "When on active duty during the period from and including August 1942 until August 1945, at Tokyo, was engaged in broadcasting and script-writing for broadcasting of Japanese propaganda over Tokyo Radio." If found guilty by the Army, he would lose his rank, and his entitlements and a dozen other allowances which he had earned.

But it all got much murkier. Lord Haw Haw in Britain had just been convicted and executed for broadcasting for the enemy. His case was quite different Cousens', but it was suggested that the same charge should apply. **That charge was one of treason.** Things suddenly got much more serious, because that charge might end in death, as it did for Haw Haw.

The Army had a problem however. Many of the charges that they were prepared to lay against Cousens were more than three years old. But there was a moratorium of three years on them. Some of the more telling charges, they thought, could not be argued. So, **the Army** preferred not to proceed.

The **Commonwealth Government** then decided to try him, but it had its own difficulties. When the Commonwealth Crimes Act was drawn up, it was not anticipated that an Australian would ever be charged with treason in a **foreign** country. So now, under Commonwealth law, a person could be indicted for treason, but only if the suspect acts were committed within Australia. So it, too, was not able to proceed.

Now **NSW** got into the act. It turned out that in the recent past, **in 1351 in fact**, when the Black Prince was striding through Europe in the Hundred Years' War, his father, Edward III enacted a statute that could be used to good effect in Australia in 1946 - 47. To charge a man with treason. The only softening of this stance was that he should be brought before a magistrate first, prior to a full trial before the NSW Supreme Court. The idea of this was to see if a prima facie case existed against him.

On July 23, 1946, Cousens was issued with a summons to appear at Central Police Court "for traitorously conniving and attempting to aid and assist the said enemies of our Sovereign Lord the King...." Despite the lowly court in which the hearings were scheduled, many of the barristers involved were to become famous, such as Dovey, Barwick, and Shand. The hearings opened on August 20, 1946. The stakes were high.

The material presented, over more than four weeks, was more or less routine. The evidence and the cross-examinations were aimed at establishing whether Cousens had been coerced, and whether he had delivered seditious material. The Prosecution made two mistakes. Firstly, it brought out two Japanese witnesses, who had been in Tokyo at the time. They were necessary for the Prosecution's case because the law stated that at least two persons had to be present at the time of the offence. But, in a period when resentment against all things Japanese was at its peak, they received a poor welcome here. The Press made a welter of it, saying that a good Australian was to be prosecuted using Japanese witnesses, even given the fact that all such persons were by definition evil liars.

The second mistake was to not actively call one particular witness who might have collaborated much of Cousens' version of events. This man, Henshaw, was still in Japan, but was immediately summonsed to appear. When he did, he supported Cousens' story. The fact that Henshaw was not initially called as a witness was seen as an attempt by the State to exclude an important source of information.

Apart from these Prosecution gaffes, the Defence made one very good point. Thousands and thousands of Australian soldiers had been forced to work on various projects for the Japanese. Some of them had refused, and some of these had been brutalised and killed. Others had not refused, and thankfully, some of these survived. Could anyone say that this was not the same position that Cousens had been in? He had, the Defence claimed, gone as far as anyone could go to defy the Japanese without severe punishment. He was no different from many others.

After due consideration, the NSW Senior Crown Prosecutor, Thomas Crawford, announced that this is "a hopeless case, and I do not consider the great publicity that has been given to the proceeding to be any justification for continuing the prosecution." On November 6, the NSW Attorney-General announced that he had decided to drop the case. The treason charge had gone away.

But **the Army and the Commonwealth** had not finished. On December 12, Berriman, GOC Eastern Command, sent a notification to Cousens stating that "you are hereby called upon **to show cause why your commission should not be cancelled**." He was given 14 days to reply. He assembled the same type of defence as before and duly submitted it.

On early 1947, the Military Board, sat in judgement, and eventually made its decision. The matter was a simple one for them. Cousens had been asked **to show cause**. If he had shown **a willingness** to go before a court-martial to clear his name, then that would have been an indication that he had nothing to hide. But he did not so apply for a court-martial **So his name could not be cleared.** The Federal Attorney General summed it up. "Above all, he has **not** requested that the charge against him should proceed to trial. I am accordingly of the opinion that the cause shown is insufficient and that Major Cousens cannot be regarded as having merited honourable retirement. It is recommended that the commission of Cousens be cancelled."

Of course, the whole logic of this is absurd. It is quite fantastic to suggest that a person, obviously already condemned by the military authorities, should volunteer to be tried by them. Here he was, after three years' imprisonment by the Japanese, and after one full year in the civil courts, expected to subject himself to another trial that would certainly take longer, and be conducted mainly in secret. Not likely.

Still, that was the final decision. Cousens could now leave the Army and get a job. He returned to 2GB. Later he spent a couple of years at Channel Seven, and after that he went to the ill-fated company, International Vending Machines.

Towards 1950, he attended the US to give evidence for Iva Toguri, Tokyo Rose, in her delayed trial. She was convicted of treason and sentenced to ten years' imprisonment. Cousens died suddenly at home in 1964, aged sixty. The large crowd that attended his funeral attested to the fact that, whatever toll his trial had taken, many thousands of people, including his old soldier mates, still respected him at the highest level.

NEWS AND VIEWS

Federal Cabinet. Restrictions on the sale of **cream** and the manufacture of **ice cream** will be lifted next Monday, the Metropolitan and Suburban Dairyman's Association announced. It said though that it was likely that dairymen would be unable to meet the householders' cream requirements. There was not enough surplus milk to produce the cream, and there was a severe shortage of bottles.

Milk and Ice Carters Union. The Secretary, Mr Thompson, said that the Government had acted stupidly in lifting bans on the sale of cream. He said that 50,000,000 gallons of milk that should be made into butter for consumption in Britain would now be used for cream here.

Department of Postwar Reconstruction. It is expected that 85 Japanese internees (in confinement since the start of the war) will be released in the near future. Most of the internees were engaged in business before the war. **They were in no way connected to the Japanese invasion of Australia**, and were in Australia at the start of hostilities.

It is also likely that 17 Chinese nationals will be similarly treated. In addition, there are 890 Germans and 14 Italian nationals still in confinement. The Germans will not be repatriated until advice is received from the Allied Commission in Germany.

JULY NEWS ITEMS

From about now, all employees of the NSW Government will move to **State awards that grant them a 40-hour working week**. This applies regardless of whether they were previously on 44-hour or 48-hours awards. Their **take-home pay will not be reduced** because of working fewer hours. Some other States have already implemented this, and all others will soon do so. **Not all employers are happy.**

News item. Some articles of clothing will require **fewer ration coupons from now**. This will please women when they buy **dresses**, and men when they get a **new suit**. **The number of stamps needed will be reduced by about 25 per cent.** Shoes and household linen will still need their earlier allocation.

News item. Surely it's Christmas. Sugar rationing will end this month....

But meat and petrol will stay rationed.

American wrestler **Chief Little Wolf** lost his bout at Sydney Stadium last night. When the National Anthem was played, the Chief **would not stand to attention**. The manager of the stadium, well-known entrepreneur Harry Miller, entered the ring, and **told the Wolf to stand still**. Wolf picked him up, and **threw him three rows back into the crowd**. Miller suffered several small injuries, and a hurt pride....

This is a reminder to readers that **wrestling and its superb showmanship was still a major draw-card in**

Australia. Also that **the national anthem was played at the start or finish of all events**, big and little.

The British Government has established **a Birth Control Research Bureau**. Its Director, Margaret Senger-Slee, has proposed that there should be a 'moratorium' on all births right across Europe and Britain for 10 years. **She is vague of how this is to be achieved.** Some of her supporters say that education is the answer, or the licencing of couples to issue issue, or that mass castrations and mass abortions should be considered....

Such extremist views were not widely accepted, but across **the western world**, there were many who argued that **adults should not bring children into the world to starve**. What could actually be done about this remained elusive....

In Australia, we were immune from such arguments. The official line was that we were desperately short of the population needed to defend this country, and that we needed to "**populate or perish**." It turned out that there were half a million ex-servicemen, and their brides, who were willing to sacrifice themselves for the nation. **Hence, the Baby Boom.**

Thousand of cartons of **cigarettes were seized from ships** in Australia's ports last month. We had no cigarette industry, and the Customs Duty was high, so there was a **good profit to be made from smuggling....**

Tobacconists were always short of stock, and they all imposed a form of **unofficial rationing that encouraged black marketing**.

THE LASH

In the middle of 1947, a number of violent assaults were reported on people in the metropolitan areas right across the nation. In Sydney, taxi drivers were especially vulnerable, with bashings and subsequent robberies becoming daily events. Thuggery was not however confined to dark, seamy districts. For example, a young man in Mosman was assaulted by a gang in broad daylight in front of many people, and then robbed of the princely sum of tuppence (say, twenty cents).

In NSW, a Justice Markell proposed that, in some cases, the lash would be an appropriate addition to a penal sentence. The lash had not been used as a deterrent in Australia for years, having disappeared in all of the States at about the start of the twentieth century. Justice Markell's suggestions stirred many passions, and some of these are reflected in the following Letters.

Letters, E Blyth. It is interesting to read that a determined effort is to be made to stamp out the wave of crime now rampant in Sydney. I expect many people recall a similar wave of crime in Fremantle during the early years of the present century.

At a time when the police almost appeared to be losing control of the situation, a Western Australian judge provided the solution to what had become a very serious problem indeed. When passing sentence of ten years hard labour on a man convicted of a vicious assault, he warned that the sentence would be a light one compared to the next he would pass for a similar crime.

The next sentence was 15 years' hard labour, and ten lashings. The judge issued a further warning that should he again be called upon to preside in a similar case, he would inflict a heavier and still more severe sentence. This warning did not act as a complete deterrent, for still another case of thug-bashing came before him, and his sentence on this occasion was 20 years hard labour and 15 lashings, to be repeated in three months. This saw the last of such crime in Fremantle. Criminal assaults disappeared overnight.

Perhaps there are still some people who regard the lash as inhuman, but it is one sure way of playing these offenders at their own game, and the means of eliminating the thug menace now in our midst. Perhaps the Judiciary will take note.

The *SMH* obviously saw this as a problem, but was in no way clear as to the solution. It came up with the following words of wisdom, condemning the crime, but offering only lukewarm support for the idea of a good thrashing.

SMH, July 24. Judge Markell's warning that, in certain cases, he will order floggings in addition to exemplary gaol sentences for violent crimes should act as a deterrent to the thugs and bashers who have reappeared on Sydney streets. The lash, generally speaking, is an outmoded and brutalising form of punishment to which the judges are reluctant to revert. But it may be the only suitable corrective to the type of ruffianism that delights in the infliction of physical injury, often in the most cowardly and wanton circumstances. Crimes of this sort must be stamped out.

The following Letter, however, left no doubt that he did not approve of lashings. He was President of the NSW Prison Reform Council, and also a Professor of Moral and Political Philosophy at Sydney University. His opinion on a number of matters was often heard, always with deep respect.

Letters, Professor A Stout. The recent demand of a section of the public for the reintroduction of the barbarous penalty of flogging as a reply to the present outbreak of violence is perhaps understandable. It proceeds from a natural emotional repugnance to the abominable nature of the crimes being committed and rationalises itself as a demand for an effective deterrent, though it is in reality, in part at least, a demand for retribution and retaliation.

Similar popular outcries have been made before in this State – for example, during the epidemic of razor slashings and gang warfare in the late 1920's – but no judge has ordered the use of the "cat" in NSW since 1905. What is new this time is a judge has announced his intention to order flogging and has been supported by a bishop and, with evident reluctance, by your recent editorial.

The Prison Reform Council of NSW, on whose behalf I write, shares to the full the general public concern about the outbreak of thuggery, and has no sympathy for the thugs. But it does most strongly question, on scientific evidence, the efficacy of flogging as a deterrent.

Such metaphorical phrases as "giving the basher a taste of his own medicine" and "talking to him in the only language he can understand" are plausible but misleading. This is borne out by statistical evidence from England, which shows that prisoners who have been flogged two or even three times have repeated the offences for which they were punished.

Nor does the fear of the lash deter in practice. The scientific evidence on this question (see for example, the chapter on Corporal Punishment in Calvert's "The

Law Breaker") strongly supports the view that flogging is useless as a deterrent.

The Prison Reform Council believes that the long-term solution lies in the more intelligent and scientific treatment of delinquency, and especially of juvenile delinquents. The short-term solution lies not in flogging but in making detection and conviction as nearly inevitable as possible by an increase in the police force and an improvement in its mobility and communications.

This letter got a response from A Martin, also a lecturer at Sydney University, and a Vice-President of the same Council that Stout presided over. Clearly, this letter reflects a minority position within the Council.

July 27. As a Vice-president of the Prison Reform Council, I desire to dissociate myself from the recent letter to your journal under the signature of Professor Stout, protesting against "the recent demand of the general public for the introduction of the lash."

In the first place, the law concerning this type of sentence – together with the death penalty – has never been repealed from the statute book of the State. Such dire punishments have conceivably been held carefully **in reserve for times of extremity**, which have not arisen in the former case till present times.

In the second place, the threatened, but not actual, reintroduction of flogging was made by Justice Markell, an eminent member of the State judiciary, whose kindliness and wide humanitarian outlook have always been outstanding.

The welfare and reform of convicted persons have always been primarily considered by him, wheresoever consistent with the protection of the community. Those appearing before him for sentence have always been allowed a chance to make good their future, under bond and a suspended sentence, whenever they have appeared to be contrite and victims of sudden temptation.

Very reluctantly then, it may be presumed, he has now threatened the imposition of flogging upon those who might in future come before him, convicted of callous bashing and thuggery with calculated intent. Like many members of the general community, he has apparently concluded that expediency at present times must take precedent over those abstract principles to which most of us in general sincerely subscribe.

The indignity of corporal punishment is abhorrent to most thinking citizens, but concern for the general welfare of the community must now receive prime consideration. On this present occasion then, I should like to be regarded as one supporting the considered opinions of a sincere and humanitarian judge, wise and practiced in the administration of penology, rather than the side of Professor Stout and the Committee, generally invoking the strict application of abstract principles.

Then there was this other letter that took exception to Professor Stout's logic.

Letters, T Joyce. Professor Stout's letter is typical of the curious logic of his band of sentimentalists, whose idea of civic service is to make easier the lot of the transgressor.

If the severity of the penalty is no deterrent, why bother to improve the means of apprehending the criminals, as he advocates. It will all be useless anyway. And the State government's intention of advocating heavier penalties for illegal possession of firearms is also surely just a waste of effort.

It is absurd to maintain that the severity of the sentence is without some deterrent effect. If the introduction of flogging in these cases is the means of preventing even one decent citizen from being cruelly battered, it would be amply justified.

Although Professor Stout sneers at metaphorical phrases, he is guilty of a cliché himself when he says brutal punishment further brutalises a man. Is the decent citizen turned into a brute by the treatment he receives at the hands of the thug? And if the demand for the lash does arise from the desire for retaliation and retribution, which are among the most deeply-rooted instincts of the human race, should this solace be denied a man who has been assaulted and perhaps maimed and disfigured for life?

One old-timer added his bit.

Your correspondent, Mr A Martin, gives the date of the last flogging as about 1900. I knew the wicked, cruel thug concerned, as well as many of his brutal associates.

I recollect that on the morning of his release from gaol, he was met by several of his "push", and, when asked how he got on, he pulled up his clean cotton shirt and said "look at my bloody back." The outcome was that he reformed, and the fear of the lash acted as a permanent deterrent upon his mates, who gave the police no further trouble.

The Letters controversy died away, simply because the learned judge did not actually see his threat carried out. The brief written conflict – there were quite a few more letters written than I have reported – showed that there was deep interest in the matter. And had a referendum been conducted on this, it is certain that each side would have gained many votes. Just as, I believe, it would if conducted now.

CANING IN SCHOOLS

In 1947, caning in schools was quite widespread, both in the public and private schools. Probably, it was used more frequently in the Catholic schools, where it was used routinely as an instrument of crowd control, rather than as a way of enforcing individual discipline. In any case, the cane and the strap were very familiar to most students.

Opposition to the use of this form of corporal punishment was always present in some parts of society, and raised its head periodically. It did so again now, and these three letters show some of the arguments for and against.

Letters, Modern Mother. May I say, in answer to "Modern Father", that as a mother of two young children, I soon found out that some children are much more easily handled than others. In our own case one child has been very little trouble, but the other child was a "nightmare," on many occasions. Cutting out a bedtime story would have no effect at all.

A highly-strung and excitable child very often does not hear but he feels. Whilst in the infants' school, this child caused a lot of trouble, but after the mistress was told to use the cane if necessary, there was no more difficulty.

I might mention that we had earlier taken him to a well-known psychologist, who, after talking to the child for some time, said "Whack him." I can now thankfully say he is almost a little gentleman, at the age of nine, and not at all repressed or broken in spirit. I maintain that the cane must be there, not used consistently, but as a deterrent.

Letters, L Gullett. I was very glad to read that the Dutch delegate to the international conference on education in Brisbane deplores the use of the cane in Australian schools. Some years ago a kindly Minister for Education tried to stop this brutal punishment, but it was again restored when he left office. Only a few weeks ago a teacher was fined for having so cruelly beaten a small boy that a doctor's attention was necessary.

I know that there are many fine men and women in the teaching community who know that violence is not necessarily needed to impart knowledge, but there are still many teachers who delight in beating small children, especially the slow, stupid, and backward ones – which, of course, makes them more stupid still.

The use of the cane should be absolutely forbidden in every school. Until this is done, there is going to be unnecessary suffering for many children.

Letters, F Rocke. Miss Gullett states that there are still many teachers who delight in beating small children.

What grounds does Miss Gullett have for such a strong statement? I have taught in four schools in both NSW and Victoria, and I have never observed such attitudes. Perhaps my experience is narrow, but I have noticed a decided tendency to minimise the use of the cane.

While individual brutality should be checked, surely it is no reason for the abolition of corporal punishment. What sensible parent would have confidence in a profession which, while doing its utmost to win the love and respect of the children, was forbidden the use of corporal punishment in extreme cases?

As a matter of fact, this problem seems to sum up the disciplinary problem of our community – detention versus corporal punishment. In our worthy efforts to be more civilised, we have forgotten that there are still uncivilised elements in our community, which can be influenced only by the infliction of pain.

The use of corporal punishment was later forbidden by the signing of the Universal Declaration of Human Rights; although, by then, the use of the cane had dropped a lot. However, I think that there would right now be a fair number in the community who believe that its **selective** use in the schools, for chronic offenders against discipline, would be justified. And, it is doubtless true, there would also be many who would oppose its use in any circumstances.

Capital punishment.   Queensland was the first State to abolish the death penalty. It conducted its last execution in 1913, and abolished the penalty in 1917. But by 1947, it was still on the Statute books in all other States.

It was not until the late Sixties and the Seventies that these States removed it. The last one to do so was NSW, which had generally gotten rid of it in 1955, but kept it as penalty for treason until 1985. The last person to be executed in Australia was Robert Ryan in Victoria in 1967.

ENGAGEMENT OF PRINCESS ELIZABETH

Congratulatory messages poured in from all parts of the world as the engagement of Princess Elizabeth was announced. Her husband-to-be was Lieutenant Phillip Mountbatten of Greece, and from the Royal Navy. The Times of London said that the pleasure of the people was greater because it is apparent that there can have been no motive but the impulse of their own hearts that brought this young couple together.

The King, George VI, has given his permission for the betrothal. It is expected that, at a later date, he will give his consent to the marriage. This is the procedure laid down in the Royal Marriage Act of 1772.

Today, after "still" photographs were taken, Phillip helped Elizabeth to don her coat, and then the couple walked, laughing and talking, along the Palace terrace, where moving pictures were taken. Both looked radiantly happy. Mountbatten, who became a British resident earlier this year, will probably move from his Greek Orthodox religion to the Church of England.

Comment. This glowing report mentions that the Princess was radiant, and I add that I agree. There were over 200 different photographs of her reproduced in the Australian papers and journals, and in every one, she looks to be on top of the world. Phillip, however, was caught a few times looking a bit disconcerted with all the publicity.

The good news was greeted jubilantly in Australia. Almost all people here were still firmly British in outlook, and wholeheartedly gave their approval and support. As it turned out, on the very day that the announcement was made, the British Government realised at last that the nation was still living beyond its means, and started to cut it costs, worldwide. It then started a process that weakened its ties to the Empire, and which ultimately led to the growth of a moderately strong republican movement in Australia. But at this time, there was no evidence of that at all, and the mood was one of general rejoicing.

Ben Chifley's message said "on behalf of the Government and people of Australia, and my wife and myself, I send loyal affectionate greetings to your Majesties, and offer to her Royal Highness, Princess Elizabeth, our felicitations and best wishes on the occasion of the announcement of her engagement to Lieutenant Phillip Mountbatten."

Almost identical messages came from every one you would expect.

The *SMH* editorial positively waxed. Under the heading, *Royal Romance*, it went on "Australians everywhere will join whole-heartedly with 530 million fellow subjects in sending a world-wide message of cordial congratulations". The editorial then rejoiced that it was a matter of the heart alone, and spoke of her charm and youthful eagerness, balanced by dignity and simplicity. It was a masterful piece of writing, and conveyed the thoughts and well-wishes of millions here.

In London, the mood was euphoric. Crowds, which had waited up to six hours outside Buckingham Palace, burst into singing when the couple appeared on the balcony. They first sang "The Sailor with the Navy Blue Eyes", and followed this up with "All the nice Girls Love a Sailor", and then "Daisy Bell".

They began a chant of "we want the King" and "we want the Queen", and these two persons came out for ten minutes and waved, we presume, majestically. Then they went inside, and left the young ones to their adulation.

At the same time, it was reported that the Princess wanted the wedding dress designers to start work as soon as possible, so that the work of dress houses for the export trade would be disrupted as little as possible.

The King got in on all this political correctness and said that he wanted as little labour and materials as possible to be diverted for **the staging of the wedding**. Nevertheless, "there is a presumption that extra staging will be needed to seat **the 2,000 guests** that will be invited. This will be over and above **the large numbers of official guests."**

Letters to the Australian Press were surprisingly few. Most of those persons who did write were quite predictable, and said all the normal things. But there was one delightful variation, that sums it all up.

Letters, A Philliss. It is great to see young Elizabeth meeting her match, and enjoying it. Years ago, when that other bloke was running round with that American divorcee, I gave the Royal Family away. I said they would never amount to nothing.

But since then, King George VI and his beautiful wife came along, and brought with them two good children. The young one is a bit snooty, but Elizabeth is great. I hope she and Phillip Mountbatten have a long and prosperous life together, and raise kids as beautiful as she is.

AUGUST NEW ITEMS

Many **Jewish populations** round the world are striving to set up **a new Jewish state** in the Arab region in Palestine. Some progress is being made by negotiation, but **armies of terrorists are** plaguing the region trying to hasten the departure of the British and the establishment of the state of **Israe**l....

It was common to read headlines such as those of August 1st. "*British Captives Hanged. Grim Reprisal by Jews.*" The story went on to say that the bodies of two soldiers were found in a grove, and that the bodies were booby trapped, as was the area round them....

Though the British did grant independence within a year, **war and terrorism has persisted in the region until this day**. Despite the way the papers talk, **terrorism has been round for a long, long time**.

Meanwhile, **another nation** was seeking to be free of colonial ties. **Freedom fighters, or terrorists if you choose,** were seeking independence from the Dutch in Indonesia. Another headline on August 1st read "*Java City in Ruins. Dutch take Malang*", a picturesque city of 100,000....

This war of armed locals fighting the reluctantly-departing Dutch was being echoed across the globe as **nationalist forces took the opportunity and seized control** from the colonial powers weakened by war. **Britain, France and Holland were the main targets.**

Two brothers, aged 9 and 5, were found **dead in their bath** at home in the NSW city of Tamworth. **Their gas**

bath-heater had gone out, and the gas continued to flow until they died of the fumes.

NSW is entering a liquor trading war. 72 new clubs were registered recently and began to trade. They were mainly ex-Servicemen's and sporting clubs. Government authorities insist that these clubs, like pubs, must close at 6pm, and not trade on Sundays....

The clubs say that this defeats the purpose of clubs which they see as **providing wider drinking hours for families, and refreshment and entertainment for weekend** sportsmen and their families....

At the weekend, inspectors visited the 72 clubs, and found them in breach of the law. No fines were imposed, but **a warning was issued to each.** This will grow into **a major dispute, that will take two decades to settle.**

Customs officers in ports are not just on the look-out for **tobacco products.** They are just as vigilant looking for **nylon stockings.** These aids to beauty are scarce, and the duty payable on each pair is substantial. So smugglers and black marketeers are again matching their wits against the Customs men, and to judge by the number of nylons on the streets from dubious men in overcoats, **the smugglers were winning.**

On Sydney's trams, a lot of fares were being lost as **conductors could not get to many travellers** because of crowding. Transport Officials tried putting four **honesty boxes on each of 13 trams.** After a trial of eight days, the average per tram was two shillings per box. **Not worth the effort.**

LIFE, AND DEATH, FOR BOYS

Mr Justice Owens, in the NSW Supreme Court, at Auburn, gave judgement on six boys all aged under 17 years, two of whom were still at school, who had been found guilty of gang rape. Prior to that, another boy aged 19 years, had been sentenced **to death** for his leading part in the crime. The younger boys were each handed out a penalty of **life imprisonment** with hard labour, under laws which made such a sentence **mandatory**. His Honour indicated that, under the Child Welfare Act of 1939, he had no choice other than to impose these penalties. He added that he would much rather have sent them to an institution, and leave officers of the Child Welfare Department to determine the length of detention. The jury also recommended against the imposition of these penalties.

Public interest in this matter was extreme, as the following writings on the matter indicate.

The Editorial from the *SMH* left no doubt about what it thought. Under the heading "Barbarous Penalty", it argued that the legal requirement for a judge, against his better will, to impose such penalties on "mere children" was "severe to the point of savagery." It points out, in the case of the young man sentenced to death, that current practice was to go through "the extreme farce" of pronouncing the death penalty, with the certain knowledge that the penalty would be remitted to life. The Editorial goes on to advocate in strong terms for the revision of the appropriate statutes, and specifically, it calls for the Executive of the Government to grant clemency to all the boys.

Letters, A McGuiness. In England, for example, rape brings with it penal servitude for periods ranging from life to not less than three years. Or it might bring imprisonment, with or without hard labour, for not more than two years. It all depends on the circumstances.

Mr McGuiness goes on to enumerate that other States and New Zealand are also less severe in their approach. He also points out that, in South Australia, no person under 18 years can be imprisoned, and it is quite difficult to send under-19s to gaol in Britain.

Letters, W Simms. This unfortunate incident and others are symptomatic of a sick community and society. Complacency, carelessness, and irresponsibility towards the young are found everywhere. Public conduct leaves much to be desired. Wolf-calling is treated as humorous instead of offensive. Far too many girls go out at night without responsible protection.

The Government, the Churches, and the populace generally must shake off their lethargy, and provide wholesome pleasures and interests for the young people on the one hand, and protect them by personal experience and vigilance on the other. This way, tragedy and remorse may be avoided.

Letters, DISGUSTED. The sentence may be a hard one, but it fits the crime. When one considers the pain that can be done to women physically and mentally, surely the punishment should be such as to make men and boys think twice before they commit the offences.

By enforcing the law, instead of mitigating the punishment, a move could be brought about to make our towns and cities safer for women.

Letters, TWO GRANDPARENTS. Thank you for your sub-leader, "Barbarous Penalty." Those in authority who remain silent over imparting true sex knowledge to adolescents placed in their care might ponder this utterance "Virtue is knowledge, vice is ignorance."

Letters, Mary Tenison-Woods. But imprisonment for life is not the remedy; education, training, treatment by competent people – this is the only treatment. ....
The graver the offence, the greater the need for more the enlightened and scientific approach of the juvenile courts, where reclamation rather than punishment is the guiding principle.

Letters, Lorna Hall. While the humanitarian outbursts on behalf of the offenders is to admired, the damning cause of the conduct must not be allowed to go unchecked.

Life is a slippery path for all young people. Sex instruction is not sufficient; protection is also necessary. Drinking at dance halls must be stopped, no matter who is offended. Indeed, the whole of the drink trade is alarming in its damage to human welfare. So-called clubs, places of entertainment, are a disgrace. We should close them all down.

Letters, Lex. You show too much sympathy for the offenders. Our women-folk must be protected, and offenders, even young ones, made to realise that rape, and mass rape in particular, is a serious offence. The spirit of lawlessness is altogether too prevalent in our community. There is also too much maudlin sympathy for the offenders when they get caught.

Letters, H Oxford. It is to be hoped that parents, who so far have been unwilling to inform their children of sex, will now face up to their responsibilities. It is wrong to fall into the all-too-common belief that sex, like general knowledge, is a matter for formal instruction at school. It is questionable whether it is, in fact, a matter for State responsibility.

The Government could possibly issue a carefully prepared booklet for parents on sex discussion, or perhaps parents who are incapable of accepting their responsibilities could approach a doctor, social worker, clergyman, headmaster/headmistress in order to arrange for a talk to be given to a boy or girl.

The real responsibility is with the home, where, generally speaking, privacy, friendship and example offer the best background to healthy and proper behaviour.

Letters, D Sands. Would it not be better to examine the causes rather than the punishments already provided by the statutes. How far do salacious movies, bathing costumes on the beaches, and pictures of semi-nude girls published in certain sectors of the Press contribute to criminal sex impulses.

While a Labor Government is in power, criminals at large, and those with an inclination to commit capital offences know that they do not need to fear the gallows, no matter how callous or horrible the atrocities that they commit or contemplate. Gallows frighten thugs.

Letters, V Benton. I consider the life sentence a waste. It will only make them hardened criminals. As a punishment, I suggest giving them a good flogging, and putting them on a farm to do hard physical work, plain diet, and good books to read until an improvement was noticed in their behaviour.

Letters, E Wrighty. I hope that future legislation will provide for the firm use of the cane in younger years, and sensible use of the lash for older criminals, rather than long terms of imprisonment. History has proved that flogging is a deterrent to thugs.

Telegram, A Walder. Father of three sons offers heartiest congratulations to Herald for its humane views regarding barbarous penalty for six boys.

A few weeks after this controversy, **legislation**, to remove the **mandatory** death penalty for rape by an **adult**, **was passed**. The new laws permitted the judge to impose whatever penalties he thought fit. The **mandatory** punishments for rape **by adolescents** were still applicable, and these included life imprisonment. **However**, this was dealt with under the Child Welfare Act, and the responsible Minister, for Education, **moved swiftly to change that Act as wel**l.

THE HARP IN THE SOUTH

The *Harp in the South* was a book written by Ruth Park – who also wrote the famous *The Muddle Headed Wombat*. It won a literary award given by the *Sydney Morning Herald,* and was published in installments in the *Herald* over a period of about three weeks.

It tells the story of an Irish-Australian family who lived in Surrey Hills in Sydney in the nineteen forties. This area was just up the hill from Central Railway Station, and was well known for its slums, crime, and poverty, and its fortress-mentality towards outsiders. The book covers a couple of years in the life of the family, going through events such as courtships, bashings, abortions, death, drunkenness, and marriage, all against a background of grinding poverty.

When published in installments, the book caused a major furore and brought forth many complaints from readers who objected to various aspects of the book. And then, there followed many letters of support. In all, the *Herald* received 173 letters, 102 in support and 71 against the publication. These letters provide a good look at the morality that prevailed at the time, and an interesting basis for comparisons with the more "'permissive" - or is it "sinful" - present.

Letters, Dorethy Courtney. As the daughter of an Irishman, I strongly resent Ruth Park's novel, with its cheap portrayal of people whose only fault is their lack of material goods. There are still people in Surrey Hills who speak correctly, and are not habitually in a semi-drunken state.

If this novel is the best that the judges were able to extract from the many entries received, then Australian literature is indeed in a very bad way.

Letters, Margaret Anderson. To think that in a young clean country (clean as compared with the older countries) such unadulterated filth should be given first prize, and put out to the world as representing Australian life, makes my blood boil.

Letters, T Taylor, Methodist Parsonage. At a largely attended meeting of the Willoughby Methodist Circuit, the following resolution was unanimously passed:

"This quarterly meeting is of the opinion that the fact that the three leading prizes have been awarded to novels that deal so largely with the sordid side of life, is detrimental to the proper observance of moral standards. If the installments already published are any criterion of the books concerned, we sincerely regret their publication."

Letters, O Farquhar. I feel that Miss Park's story is so true to life and her atmosphere is so right that it must do more good than harm.

May it do as much good as "Oliver Twist", Kingsley's "Water Babies", "Uncle Tom's Cabin" and numerous others that have proved that the pen is mightier than the sword.

The foregoing stories are not pretty by any means, but they have done more good for the under-privileged than years of legislation could ever do.

Letters, Nina Lowe. Many critics who are not opposed to "realism in literature" do not hesitate **to accuse a woman**, forced by our economic system to live in the slums, and who by her brilliant writing has made that sordid quarter spring to a life which breaks in upon our pharisaical complacency, **of using a muck-rake**.

Well, what implement does one use to shift muck? Or is the implied counsel to leave it lie, fouling and fermenting in the heart of our city?

Letters, Croyde Whiffen. I admire Ruth Park for her courage in speaking out. There is too much hush-hush over "facts" which, if spoken of freely, would perhaps make a cleaner and saner community.

One critic said "Why bring dirt and squalor before us all when there are so many beautiful places in the world and also love?" This is the most selfish thing that anyone could say. I daresay that there is as much hidden under some of these beautiful places as there are in a slum area like Surrey Hills, and with far less excuse.

Letters, ANOTHER CRITIC. If "The Harp in the South" is a sample of literary merit, then one can only view with disgust and alarm the retrograde step that Australian authorship has taken.

The easy and blasphemous use of the name of God, the thinly-veiled references to vulgar expressions, and the description of the amorous conduct of a young couple in the park, make very sordid reading, and can do nothing but corrupt the minds of those who indulge in it. Must our literary talent dig deep into cesspits to produce mental food for the people? Where are our censors that such writings are allowed to become part of our literary possessions?

Letters, Harold Grant. The novel is a refreshing taste of reality, and is a smack in the eye for those who abhor the other side of the fence. The critics who are revolted by the seamy, yet factual, delineation of real life should cast aside their scented handkerchiefs, travel into not-so-well-known areas, browse round a bit, and vigorously inhale the odours that a health inspector would not pass.

Letters, SATISFIED READER. Cannot people look at this question from the point of the book's obvious merits and very entertaining plot. Although the material is necessarily sordid, the characters are extremely well drawn, and presented by someone who obviously knows what she is writing about.

It makes entertaining reading, and is one of the best newspaper serials that I have ever read. As for effects on overseas readers, would anyone take "The Grapes of Wrath" as a true presentation of American life?

Letters, R Coombe. It is regrettable that the best novel in the Herald's literary competition should be such a sordid one. Why should this nation with all her beauty to choose from, have to go to the sewer for her literature.

Letters, J Brown. I think that the Harp in the South is disgusting and revolting. Why does Ruth Park single out one suburb, one nation, and one religious denomination. I have friends living in Surrey Hills, and in the speech and manners and morals compare favourably with those living in other parts of Sydney.

I don't think any good regarding slum clearance will come out of this book. It will be appreciated only by those who like their reading sordid – or worse.

Summing up: Critics said that the book would debauch the impressionable, and that it presented Australia in a bad light, and there was some swearing and blasphemy. Looking from **today's perspective, none of these charges have much foundation**, but – put into the context of 1947 – they were obviously quite serious for many people. In today's literary scene, the "offensive" writings would pass almost unnoticed.

The defenders of the book say the above charges were – for them – trivial, and that its value lay in revealing the **social and economic problems** that the story pointed to. It represented a call to action, to alleviate the problems of the down-trodden who went on from generation to generation in a squalor that was impossible to escape.

Behind these immediate matters, there was another battle starting. And that was **over realism in Australian literature**. Many critics objected to the starkness of the situations presented, and would clearly have liked a sugar-coated version. "Would anyone care to see it **acted**, and listen to the ghoulishly described screams of the unfortunate girl at No. 177? I think not."

This is a battle that has continued on over the last half century, and for all the many blows landed, there is as yet no winner. There are many readers now who get so much so-called realism in their escapism, particularly from television, that they welcome the omission of sordid writing. Then again, there are others who think the best parts of books are the grotty bits. I suppose all you can say is that realism is now here to stay, and the reader has the choice as to what to read. But how does anyone know what's in a book until they read it? Perhaps, through book reviews, or by word of mouth. But anyway, now there is an unending supply of realism if anyone wants it.

NEWS AND VIEWS

Letters, PATRON. I read with considerable astonishment a report that, under the new State Liquor Act, licenses had been refused for two well-known restaurants because "if licences were extended to two restaurants with **fixed seats** in alcoves, sexual passions would be excited." For one of the restaurants concerned, it stated that patrons might go there for the purpose of "sidling up to strangers."

What is this odd thing of sidling up? I have travelled fairly extensively and dined in many diverse types of cafes, and I have never yet come into contact with a person who practices the peculiar art of sidling up to a fixed-in seat.

All that the Licensing Board have done is to deprive two highly respectable Sydney restaurants of the long-overdue boon of a liquor licence. Its members can now rest on their laurels, secure in the knowledge that they have protected a small section of Sydney society from the untold horrors of the built-in seat. The whole episode would be amusing if it were not so insulting to our intelligence.

SEPTEMBER NEWS ITEMS

The **British Government is** so worried about its balance of payments problems that it **has forbidden overseas travel for pleasure for all persons.** One such person is **Princess Elizabeth** who, with new husband-to-be Prince Phillip, **was planning a honeymoon trip to Norway** at the invitation of the King of Norway....

Authorities have decided that **no exception will be made for the Princess**, and so they will honeymoon in a country house in the south of England. Next year they will go overseas, probably to **New Zealand**, but that will be **seen as a duty and not for pleasure.**

Australian authorities too are worried about our balance of payments. They have imposed cuts on overseas expenditure. For example, overseas entertainers and sportsmen will have **a limit of one thousand Pounds on what they can send back home**. That will just about cut off all such visitors. Another example is that our overseas travellers will see **a reduction of 30 per cent on what money they can take with them**....

Imports of **tobacco** will be cut by a further 20 per cent. Imports of **cars** by an equal amount. **The list goes on.**

Certain provisions of the war-time National Security Regulations **forbade mid-week horse racing events, and betting on night trotting**. These provisions are due to **expire at the end of this month**....

The NSW Government has decided to extend them for at least 15 months, **"because of the need to provide supplies of building materials."** The link between building supplies and the horse racing industry eluded most people. **Cartoonists had a field day** showing horses pulling waggons in brick quarries being withdrawn in time for the First at Randwick....

Many commentators suggested that the decree had nothing to do with the supply of materials, but was **an expression of the power of those churches that opposed gambling.**

As India edges closer to independence from Britain, the formation of a separate State of Pakistan is approaching. **Riots in India** in the last few weeks have increased, and the **Moslems are fighting against the Hindus** in cities and villages across the nation. **Gandhi started a fast** to highlight the violence and try to stop it.....

But he called it off after only 58 hours, because he was warned by the British that if he died or suffered serious damage, "**40 million Moslems inside India will pay a horrible price in blood.....**"

Millions of people are **moving out of India and into Pakistan, and millions are moving the other way** with huge chaos and violence. For example, in Sialkot in the new Moslem State, 120,000 Hindus were due to evacuate. After battles, only 1,500 survived. **Comment. Such atrocities are being reported every day.**

A thought. In 1947, most weddings were conducted **inside** churches. Seventy years later, I suspect that many more are conducted **outside** churches. Am I correct?

What about funerals? Buried or cremated?

WOOMERA

In September, various whispers leaked deliberately by the Federal Government, pointed to the likelihood of parts of the Australian desert being commandeered for use as a testing ground for British rockets. It was argued in official circles that rockets would be used in future wars as a means of bombing enemies, and that, by collaborating with the British, Australia could leap to the forefront in this new technology. It was further argued that our deserts were sparsely occupied, and that the few inhabitants would be readily moved out of danger.

At the same time that this deal was being considered, Australia was also jockeying to get into the *atom bomb club*, which then consisted of the USA, and Britain, and also Canada to some extent. Our politicians were most anxious to gain bomb technology, and indeed for decades tried all sorts of deals to gain atomic bomb secrets. Part of the thinking then was that if we could get access to rocket secrets by collaborating with the British, it would smooth the way for a similar arrangement for atom bombs. And **apparently** it did, for early in the 1950's, Australia joined Britain in testing a number of atom bombs, again in the deserts. Without giving the story away for readers of later volumes in this series, I add that our vision of getting atomic secrets was frustrated at every stage by American interests, and to this day we have no indigenous military nuclear capability.

Opposition to the rocket proposal was muted, initially. It seemed too far away to bother a population that was mainly living on the coastal fringe. And perhaps it would not happen. But late in 1947, the Government announced that trials would proceed, and gave **some scant details**.

The target area was to start in South Australia and stretch to the north west coast of Western Australia and beyond. The mainland component was 1100 miles long and 120 miles wide, and went out another 1900 miles over the Indian Ocean to Christmas Island. Because this project was classified as defence related, inevitably further information was almost impossible to get. This remained the case over the many years of testing, and it was not until the 1980's, during the enquiries into the atom bomb tests, that a little more light was thrown onto the matter. But not **much** more.

At this stage, there were two issues that stood in the way of a widespread public protest. **Firstly**, there was the strong sentiment that we were part of the British Empire, and that if Britain wanted anything, we should give it. **Secondly**, white Australia's attitude to the Aborigines was still ambiguous, and their welfare – to many – was a matter of no concern. But there was a heightened outcry, and the Letters below reflect this. The first three Letters were written in September, when the leaks were occurring. The others appeared as more plans were announced.

Letters, F Ferrier. West of the overflow of the Hay River in the Northern Territory, in the waterless waste of the uninhabited Simpson desert, there is an ideal 200 miles square for a rocket bomb target where, even in the seldom recurrent wet season, it would be impossible to injure anything except an odd rabbit or emu. This is probably the most useless piece of country on earth, from a human habitation point of view.

When I pioneered it thirty years ago, I found that blacks only entered it in wet seasons in search of pituri, a native narcotic. The area contained nothing but lines of waterless, almost uncrossable sandhills, uninhabited, and as far as I could ascertain, never from the dawn of time inhabited. Between the uncrossable sandhills lies a profusion of claypans, ideal landing grounds for observation planes. For bomb tests, Australia has in the Simpson Desert the goods.

Letters, Michael Sawtell, Aboriginal Welfare Board, Sydney.

I wish to add my voice to those which are protesting against using inland Australia for a bomb alley. Years ago, prospectors used to go out from Laverton, Western Australia, and in the dry season they would capture **a wild native**, tie him up, feed him on salt beef, and keep him from water. When they thought him thirsty enough, they would ask the native, "Which way water?" The Aborigine would then go through great thirst before he would disclose the whereabouts of water, because the place of tribal soaks was a tribal secret.

The firing of bombs over inland Australia might easily destroy these native soaks. The few scattered Aborigines might not be able to find or go to other soaks because they might be out of their tribal grounds and in the keeping of a hostile tribe. I am one of the very few men in Sydney who have ever been in Simpson, so I know what a real native soak is like.

Letters, C Mountford. The proposal to use a portion of the Aboriginal reserve as a test range for rocket bombs is frightful, but I am sorry to say, quite in line with our past treatment of these people. I know the reserves over which it is proposed to send the rockets very well, probably better than any other white man. For months on end while investigating their customs and beliefs, I traveled and lived with these people on their own land, and I can say with certainty that there are few, if any, places in the reserves where, at one time or another, the Aborigines do not travel or camp. They would be in continual danger from falling bombs.

But why use the Aboriginal reserves at all. Surely, there are enough empty spaces in Australia where a test range could be laid out that would not pass over the Aboriginal reserve or inhabited areas; Simpson Desert, west of Tennant's Creek, or north from Kalgoorlie, to name a few.

It always seems impossible to prevent munitions makers and the military minds from playing with these death-dealing weapons, which every thinking person knows will, if persisted in, finally destroy our civilisation. But in the last mad race towards that awful end, let us, at least, keep our word to the Aborigines and leave their reserves inviolate.

Letters, (Rev) R Hickin, National Missionary Council of Australia: The whole question of the proposed rocket tests in Central Australia has been discussed by the missionary boards of the Protestant Churches of Australia.

The choice of the area as announced is highly undesirable as it would mean the violation by whites of an area which has hitherto been able to ensure to the Aborigines freedom from interference.

Further, the Aboriginal belief in a spirit relationship with particular localities makes movement of the groups to another area impracticable.

Although the area chosen by the British Military Mission may be the best that could be found, questions such as the foregoing must not be overlooked, from the viewpoint of humanity, it would be better to choose a second-best site. In any case, the Government should admit its responsibility to recognise Aboriginal rights and should provide, when establishing any such stations, that white men are excluded under heavy penalties from entering Aboriginal reserves except under special licence in each individual case for a particular purpose.

Dr Martyn's letter in the Herald suggests that scientific discovery is far more important than Aboriginal life, and it is against such a view that the National Missionary Council feels it must lodge a vigorous protest.

Letters, INTERESTED. The moving of a few wraith-like skeletons from the Central Australian area is a sin that will rest but lightly on our shoulders, in comparison with **the sins of omission and oppression we have perpetuated on them.** We have forced the black man to live as a sort of pariah, doing menial work and existing on scraps from the white man's table.

The Aboriginal is backward, but like any other human being, he will respond to fair and decent treatment, as many of the missionaries and we in the Army proved. The question is a difficult one, but it could be solved by proper education on a large scale, combined with rights of free citizens, in an atmosphere that contains more tolerance than in which he exists today. I wonder if the Four Freedoms will ever get as far as the Territory?

Surely, it is somewhat inconsistent for so much consideration to be devoted suddenly to the welfare of the Aborigines, when a policy of slow extermination has been so successfully carried out over the years.

On November 30, reacting to public consternation at the project, Mr Dedman, the Minister for Post-war Reconstruction, issued some reassurances. He claimed that there would generally be only one firing per week, and that for some years, the range would be limited to a point short of the Aboriginal reserves. "Reports that huge areas in Central Australia will be blasted by explosions are highly-coloured figments of the imagination." The risk to an individual Aborigine would be less than that involved in crossing the street. He went on to point out that, by its involvement, Australia would make a large contribution towards the defence of the Empire, and strengthen the security of the British Commonwealth by providing for the dispersal of our weapons over many international sites.

Mr Dedman's statement failed to mollify. The following year, and indeed for many years, resistance increased, but to no avail. The tests went ahead, always under a shroud of secrecy. It is hard to see any material advantage that we got from co-operating with the British in this matter. Certainly, **we did not get to join the nuclear club**, and also any rocket knowledge we gained is not apparent today. It is not at all clear just how much damage was done to Aborigines. The governments since, through a number of enquiries, have maintained that there was no damage. On the other hand, groups of Aborigines say the results were substantial. Even in 2008, there were claims being made before the courts for compensation. I have the feeling that the claimants in these latter cases were justified, but, unfortunately – tragically – we will probably never find out.

SILK STOCKINGS

One of the big fashion industry questions being asked in mid-1947 was "when will silk stockings become available?" David Jones ran a large advertisement seeking to answer this question. It said the answer to the question was that there was no answer.

The giant store explained that the supply of silk yarn was very small, and erratic, and nothing was dependable. Given only a trickle of supply, it meant that all retailers had to ration sales. With this, "no one is more disappointed than David Jones."

It goes on to spell out its policy for distributing this product. One way would be to put the stockings up for sale as soon as they come in, and just let them go in a rush to anyone who happened to be there to buy them. Rather it proposes to release its allocation "in small parcels at odd times each day." That means that anyone buying stockings then, in any of these short unspecified periods, will be able to get a pair. It goes on to say that this situation will continue for some time. It also adds that it may be some time before it can make any comment on **nylon** stockings.

This, of course, was a good marketing ploy. It meant that desperate women would loiter round the stores for quite a while each day until the stockings came on sale at the unspecified periods. This would no doubt be good for sales of other products. But the whole advertisement shows just how anxious ladies were to get these stockings at a time that was now almost two years from the end of the war.

NEWS AND VIEWS

Letters, A Penfold. Most housewives have been without washing soap and powders for several months. If there are adequate supplies of tallow and other raw material, as contended, the shortage must be due either hoarding or extra export.

It would appear also that manufacturers are producing toilet soaps in preference to washing soaps by reason of the enhanced price. Supplies of toilet soap, with which the stores are loaded today, could be reduced considerably until supplies of washing soap become available.

I object to the failure of any single authority to give an explanation of why this situation has developed, and why it persists. Has the cat got their tongue? I also object to the passive acceptance of this situation. Women have had a raw deal over the past six years, and I see no reason to make their lot harder by depriving them of washing soap.

Letters, P Bruton. There is no shortage of tallow in Australia, as ample stocks can be bought on the black market. If manufacturers purchase on this market, they cannot afford to make cheap laundry soap. Some tallow manufacturers are hoarding the tallow against the time when the Government will withdraw the prohibition against exporting it. Instead of getting twenty Pounds a ton for it now in Australia, they would get any price they asked for if it was exported to countries where tallow is in short supply.

OCTOBER NEWS ITEMS

Interstate shipping was still a viable industry in Australia. Any Company in Brisbane, say, could send goods to Perth with no more hassle than sending it by rail. The small cargo ships also **carried a handful of passengers** who could take the slower but adventurous path around the nation. **How very romantic**....

In 1947, the workers on these ships were sadly caught up in **the national sport of striking**, and anyone involved was happy to walk off the job at no notice. Often it was associated workers, such as wharfies, who did so, but ships engineers were the likely lads at the moment....

In any case, **over the next decade, such conduct blindly continued** while at the same time, **other forms of land and air transport became more competitive**. The result was that, by the end of two decades, **interstate shipping had virtually disappeared**, and that remains the case today. **Comment. What a pity.**

An interesting dodge in the war over Club closing hours. The Full Supreme Court of NSW judged that clubs could serve liquor after normal pub hours and on Sunday **if they did so in lounge areas but not in bars**. **Whacko, say the clubs**....

They are quickly buying **a few yards of red carpet** and laying it on their floor, and erecting signs round it saying "Lounge Area."

A **prominent Harley Street specialist in London** is advocating that **Britain withdraw from the 1948 Olympic Games**. This is because "her contestants are

too low in fat and protein, and would face the prospect of muscle breakdown. **Although Britons are always good losers**, it would be better to withdraw than face inglorious defeat."

Air travel, very subdued during the war, **is taking off right across the nation**. Proof of the rising popularity is that the Government has allowed **a fare increase of 20 per cent** on all flights within Australia.

During the war, Russia was considered an ally because it was fighting against Germany. Since then, it went back to its pre-war standing of international villain and bad-guy. **In Australia, our main concern was the Communist Party**, and by late 1947 dozens of propaganda machines were pumping out anti-Red material. Some of this was undoubtedly defamatory, but because of the Reds' penchant for causing strikes, **much of it was starting to stick....**

Right now, **all the other political Parties were in full cry against Communism,** both here and abroad. The artful **Bob Menzies**, as Leader of the Opposition, was coming to the fore of these attacks, and was **developing** his anti-Red policies that got him through the next 20 years of politics. **His "Reds under the Beds" theme always got him votes when he needed them.**

In October, at the age of 13, I got my first sloppy joe. You all remember what these were, so I don't need to tell you. In any case, it had a *Coat of Arms* on the front, supported by a kangaroo **and a lion**, would you believe. **It was pure magic.**

SOCIAL ISSUES

Medical Issues. The British Medical Association (BMA), was the representative body that spoke for doctors in Australia. It was not until 1962 that the **Australian Medical Association** was declared an independent body. Now, in 2020, one of its tasks is to influence the number of doctors that enter the profession, and it is always careful to ensure that the field is not oversupplied, and generally it is true that there are not enough doctors here.

Back in 1947, the problem was a different one, as this news item recounts.

State Branch of BMA. Restrictions on the entry of students to the Faculty of Medicine at Sydney University appeared to be the only way to avoid what might be **a serious surplus of doctors**, the Secretary, Dr John Hunter, said last night.

> If students continue to enter medicine at the present rate, there will undoubtedly be more doctors than the community requires. At present, there are 600 in first-year medical training alone. The total for the first three years would probably be 1,000.
>
> These are abnormal figures, and far exceed the ordinary requirements. Parents will have to decide whether it is worthwhile for their children to enter medicine with its long years of training and **the possibility, perhaps, of very little return at the end.**

Dr Hunter said that normally the community needed 40 to 50 new doctors each year. Country areas might be able to absorb more if the medical practitioners were assured of a reasonable income.

There were other worries inside the medical industry. The Chairman of the Hospitals Commission, Dr Lilly, said that practically every hospital in Sydney and in the country is still suffering from a desperate shortage of trained nurses and domestic staff. As a result, many hospitals are unable to use beds for which there is an urgent demand. Long hours of overtime worked by nurses to keep hospitals going have led to widespread complaints. The shortage is expected to persist for at least a year.

He added that the shortage was a natural aftermath of the war. It had reached these proportions because for five years of the war young women, from whom nursing trainees normally would have been drawn, had entered the women's services and they were not back yet. Normal conditions, in which girls of 18 would look to the hospitals as a means of entering an important and dignified profession, had not yet returned. "It is assumed that most of these are having a well-earned holiday, and when this is over, will again seek re-employment". Others had married and have given up their profession for good.

Dr Lilly stated that the system of training nurses in NSW could be overhauled with advantage to the hospital system and to nurses generally. He considers that trained nurses with considerable experience should be more adequately paid, but that conditions for trainee nurses compare more than favourably with the conditions for girls of a similar age in other industry.

Dr Lilly might have been correct in this latter statement. But this announcement from **Sydney Hospital** tells us that nursing was **not** a great job, at least by today's standards.

The **reduction** of nurses' working week **to 44 hours,** which came into effect today, would, it was hoped, attract more trainees into the profession, the President, Sir Norman Paul, said yesterday.

Over the years, nurses have struggled to get better conditions. But it seems that they always have to do battle for everything they get. It would be nice for them to get the occasional free-kick.

Religious issues. Most of the population **today** accept as fact that religion plays a much smaller role in society than it used to. Church attendances are down, television each day **no longer closes** each channel with a blessing from the clergy, near nudity and swearing and violence are tolerated in cinemas and in the world around us. These and other signs of the "emancipation" from religion are now commonplace. Things have certainly **changed since 1947**. For example, **then**, all the Catholic schools and convents were staffed by clergy, whereas **today**, they are run by lay teachers.

Back in 1947, in a new world just starting to feel good about itself, religion took a beating. Mind you, it still had the power to control and affect the lives of a good part of the population, and its influence could be seen at marriages, and at deaths, and at christenings, to name a few. But things were starting to change; the resistance to religion was in its infancy, but was causing alarm. The following Letters express some of this.

Letters. W Armstrong wrote in the style of the times.

A report in your paper states that church pews are empty because of gabbling through prayers, perfunctory sermons, and overpowering choirs. Can anyone seriously believe that these are the true facts of the case. If they do, then their self delusion is to be marvelled at.

The dogmas and limitations of the church in the Middle Ages will not, cannot, satisfy the awaking aspiring mind of present day humanity. Dogmas may no longer hold pride of place, and hell fire no longer be thundered from the pulpit, but what is given to the people in their place to stir their souls? Vague generalisations and pathetic, pious aspirations for the most part.

When the churches have the courage and the vision to lay the axe to the root of the tree – when their dignitaries cast aside their limitations, their prejudices, and their fears – then, and only then, will saddened clerics no longer gaze at empty pews, for man is inherently good, and "the cry of the human heart is ever for that Divine life whence it sprung."

Letters, W Arthur. The principal reason for the generally admitted increase in empty church pews is a simple one, but rarely published. It is that more and more men and women, but principally men, no longer believe in the fundamental doctrines on which the churches have built their ethical superstructures.

Putting it plainly, the virgin birth of Christ, the doctrine of the Trinity, the resurrection of Christ and his bodily ascent into heaven are less believable in an age in which reason is the test applied to postulates of all kinds, and not emotional "faith." The great power the churches might exercise by preaching the simple moral principles taught by Christ, they weaken by associating with the dogmas which reasoning man cannot accept, and they therefore are losing contact with those men whose minds have outgrown the limitations imposed by the churches.

A few clergy had their own ideas. The Rev Eastman decried the status of religion in today's society. "Many people have lost the ability to think in religious terms. They should have the Gospel message proclaimed more often in their own language **with the aid of cinema**, where practicable."

Professor Haultain Brown said that the Church did have a vital contribution to make to the preservation of civilisation. Only five per cent of the population was vitally concerned with doing Christian work. He suggested that religion required well-conceived publicity and team work. **Just as cricket and football teams visited various suburbs, so teams of spiritual advisers should visit the parishes.**

Sex Offenders. The next letter shows a remarkable shift in attitude towards sex offenders. Today, hardly a day goes past without some revelation about pornography or pedophilia. Past offenders, when they are released from gaol, are often hounded out of suburbs if the details of their crimes are revealed to their neighbours. This letter suggests a completely different attitude.

> **Letters, Compassion, Granville**. Now that the spotlight is on gaol releases, it is to be hoped that consideration will be given to the question of humane treatment of sex offenders. At the present time, there is no institution or hospital where such persons may receive treatment, and when convicted, there is no alternative to a prison sentence.
>
> It is a national disgrace that these persons do not receive special treatment for the mentally sick, which will enable them to see their mistakes and educate them to take their place in society.

The issue of education. The President of the NSW Public Services Association, Mr Tout, attacked the NSW education system and standards. "Children are growing up ill-mannered boors, with little respect for their parents, neighbours, or themselves, but they have a full knowledge of their own rights."

He went on to say that **lack of proper religious education** is mainly responsible. He questioned whether teachers are being properly trained at the colleges and universities. He asks, "are the professors in this country real teachers or learned clowns, political tools, or pseudo-experts? Don't forget the professors are the product of Government systems which seem to be drifting away from real culture."

The police and gambling. Gambling has always had an appeal to the Australian male. Immediately post-war, hundreds of thousands of these men were loose in the community, with their pockets full of pay that had been deferred and held in kitty for them till the war was over. So all forms of gambling were rife. SP betting was everywhere in every pub in the nation every Saturday. Two-up schools were almost as common, and betting on the Monday night fights was also good sport. The fact that such gambling was illegal, and constantly attracted the attention of the police, made it all the more spicy and enjoyable. Here we have a report about baccarat schools in Sydney.

The police Prosecutor, Sergeant Goode, said that the Department and the State Government were most concerned about the baccarat schools being conducted in Sydney. They had a most demoralising effect, as they brought respectable citizens into contact with big-scale racketeers.

His statement was issued from Central Police Court after 25 men and nine women were fined five Pounds each for playing baccarat at a flat in Roslyn Gardens, Darlinghurst on Tuesday night last.

When police entered the premises, a game was in progress. Most of the defendants were sitting at a long table covered by a green baize cloth. Playing cards and other implements were on the table. A sum of 35 Shillings on the table was seized by police. They were told, "You were a bit unlucky. You were a few seconds too late. You would have got at least 200 Pounds then".

Sergeant Fleming said that baccarat schools had flourished during and since the war. Great difficulty was met in efforts to get evidence about the people in control. They took every precaution by changing their location every night, employing cars to take players from one location to another, and employing scouts to keep watch for the police. He said those in control had unlimited finance, and took a commission from the players.

Divorce. Right now, in the year 2017, there is a legion of men and another legion of women who say they were dudded by divorce and by the legal and judicial system that goes with all the deliberations.

But back in 1947, all the rules were very different. For example, the Court showed that an Irene Baskill was granted decree nisi on the ground that her husband had been in a relationship with another woman. The other woman was listed as **co-respondent** in the court lists, and later the Court found in favour of the ex-wife in the disposition of all property.

Then a Kate Marshall was found to have been guilty of adultery, and similarly treated. It is interesting to reflect on the term **adultery**, because it now seems to be almost dropping out of our vocabulary. Likewise, how many **co-respondents** have you heard of recently. All of this changed a lot when Gough Whitlam came to power in 1972, and he legislated for no-fault divorce. In any case, in the past the rules pertaining to divorce were a lot tougher than they are now.

I now raise another matter that has almost completely disappeared. **Breach of promise.** In August, a Supreme Court judge awarded 125 Pounds to Susan Chandler of Maroubra, plaintiff, aged 46, in a suit for breach of promise against Laurie Coy, aged 60, of Kensington.

A few months later, Judge Markell, in the District Court, awarded a man ten Pounds and one Shilling for breach of promise. The Judge said that this differed from any other case he had come across, because the plaintiff was a man. The claim had been for 400 Pounds.

Roy Ritter had met his fiancée in Crookwell, and they had agreed to get married. He had given her 20 Pounds for a wedding dress, and she had then returned to Sydney. A few months later, when he arrived in Sydney to get married, she had told him that she was "finished." He protested, but she was adamant. Consequently, he sued for breach.

I think that in today's courting scene, where relationships often come and go quickly, it is just as well for the Court system that the offence has lapsed. South Australia formally abolished relating laws in 1971, and breach actions now in other States under the Common Law are few and far between.

Smuggling. It seems strange that this was a social issue. But the black market under rationing was so profitable that all manner of goods were smuggled all over the place. Here, we see that even the beautiful South Australian whiting was not safe.

> Large scale smuggling operations of SA whiting, by Victorians in South Australia, have been revealed by a swoop by special investigators of the Price Commission at Thevanard. Persons involved will be prosecuted.

> Inspectors said the black market prices in Victoria were 10 shillings a pound, while the official price was four shillings and fourpence. Also, they said, SA whiting travelled much better that other species. During the spying operation, inspectors camped out for more than a month, living off tinned food. At one stage they all got ptomaine poisoning. Similar pouncing operations were held at various locations along the west coast of SA.

NEWS AND VIEWS

This letter is a reminder that the Bundles for Britain programme was still working, and still very much appreciated.

> **Letters, Margaret Murray.** Britain is trying to prevent an onrush of influenza during and following the exceptional hardships of this bitter winter. Never has the psychological value of human bonds been so urgent as now, and the effect on sick persons' spirits of personal food parcels from members of more fortunate countries is shown by the following extracts from an air letter.

"Today is Sunday and, because of the great freeze-up, bundles were delivered today. You will never be able to understand the joy of receiving a food parcel from you, for the sight of its contents very nearly cured me of my influenza. Never can we remember such cold, and with no coal at home, it is hard to fight illness, try as one may. But I am starting on your **welcome tin of golden syrup** at once, and this note is to let you know what the sight of a parcel from Australia has done for me already. **During the worst of the bombing, things were never as bad here as they are today.**"

TUBERCULOSIS

The TB epidemic in Australia was in its infancy in 1947. For years, medical authorities had sent TB patients to the Blue Mountains near Sydney on the basis that the clear crisp air would work wonders for them.

But the Blue Mountains are **a death-trap for advanced cases of TB**, said Dr John Hughes, of NSW Department of Health. He said westerly winds and extreme cold would only do damage to advanced sufferers. He could not understand how this myth had gained such public acceptance. He was addressing a meeting of Health professionals in Bathurst. The meeting agreed to do a survey of the surrounding area to check the incidence of TB in the region.

NOVEMBER NEWS ITEMS

The Labor Government had been in power for most of the war years, and had introduced thousands of rules and regulations that placed **the control of the economy in the hands of the Government**. Whatever the many deserved criticisms, these policies did well enough in wartime....

So, stalwarts in the Labor Party wanted to continue them after the war. Right now, **it was attempting to pass legislation that would nationalise the banks**. That effectively meant that **the Commonwealth would be the only bank**, and that all the other banks would cease to service customers. The Labor argument is that "having a bank on every corner" is wasteful....

Opponents of the proposal say that it **denies freedom of choice**, and leaves customers facing **a government monopoly** which would inevitably bring about inefficiency and officious behaviour....

This battle is in its infancy, but is getting hot.

A different wedding present. The Aga Khan was the Imam of the Nizari Ismali community in India, and was pushing for a separate Pakistan State. He was a very rich person, and was well known on the world stage as **a person of influence and pelf**....

With **Princess Elizabeth's wedding approaching**, he elected to give her a present. **This took the form of a racehorse, a finely-bred filly.** After some consternation, the Palace announced that it would be happy to accept the gift. In 1950, it **did** win a race at Ascot.

The Melbourne Cup is a few days away. The correct attire for men is said to be **a topper, striped trousers, cravat, and patent leather shoes**....

Hiraji, **winner of the Melbourne Cup, was almost disqualified after the race.** After the dismounted jockey was on his way to the weighing-in room, a spectator, full of enthusiasm, grasped his hand and wanted to shake it. This infringed the rules that say the **jockey must not have physical contact with any person** until he has been officially weighed. **The penalty is disqualification**....

The breach was overlooked in this case because it was clearly not suspicious, and because it was brief. **And, doubtless, because it would have caused a riot.**

People were talking about restrictions on tertiary education. University education in Australia was hard to get. There were **some** scholarships, and **some** large Corporations sponsored students. But in general, most students were from rich backgrounds, **and a degree was a sign of membership of an elite....**

This was to change in 1951 when the new Prime Minister **introduced Commonwealth Scholarships** that provided free university education for **thousands** of poor but worthy students....

I am happy to say, appreciatively, that **I was one beneficiary of these**, and without this, I could never have escaped the coalfields.

Do you remember **Lifesavers and Steam Rollers?** Well, in 1947, they were back in the shops with **spritzy variations as well.**

DID CRICKET SURVIVE THE WAR?

Not only did cricket survive, it came back to Australia fully rejuvenated after the tragedy of the final test in 1938. At that time, England, in a match where no time limit was imposed, ground away to a score of over 900, with Len Hutton alone responsible for 364. So, despite all the valour that the Aussie team could muster, it lost by an innings and a lot of runs. Not a good way to start a war.

But now it was all forgotten. The Brits came back to Oz in **November, 1946**, and a five-Test series was held. **At the time**, the excitement in this nation was electric. It was such a relief to have these circuses back on the agenda, where most people ignored the frustrations of finding coupons to buy shoes, and instead spoke of the giants of the turf and the villainy of England. The air-waves were flooded with all the ifs and buts of things to come.

The papers were full of pictures of the Poms: Dennis Compton riding a bullock in Gympie; and of Compton and Edrich at the Flemington races looking like two first-class well-heeled spivs; and of captain Wally Hammond hob-nobbing with the vice-regals. What a pity he was a professional.

The Australians got even more press coverage. Ray Lindwall played in the Sydney Rugby League Premiership semi-finals, and here he was, a month later, playing cricket for Australia. Keith Miller missed most of the selection period because he flew out to marry his war-time sweetheart in America. Don Bradman might play, or then again, he might not. He would have a game of two with

South Australia, and then decide. But then, to everyone's relief, yes, he will be playing.

This excitement spilled over into 1947. So that with the cricket season about to re-start, the Letters pages of all newspapers were full of cricket. Neville Cardus started the ball rolling. He was a famed *ABC* music commentator, well known for his unshakable cricket zealotry for England, who could stir up more Australian wrath than Adolf Hitler. He made a few typically old-school and stuffy remarks about maintaining the traditions of cricket, and unleashed the flood of correspondence that I have sampled below. The reader will find that here is one aspect of life that never changes, in that there is an endless supply of people with all sorts of suggestions for a better game of cricket. Some of them are silly, some are clearly not thought out. Some of them even anticipate a number of changes that were later introduced.

> **Letters, Kenneth Henderson.** Surely with cricket, all is not unalterably for the best. Surely cricket must **continue to lose to tennis the young men** who, cooped up all week, want to be sure of exercise on Saturday afternoon.
>
> In this moment of keen and glamorous anticipation, we forget marathon tests when sides with 500 or 600 runs on the board have gone on scoring at the rate of a run about every two minutes. That last Test in England? Mental, moral, and physical breakdowns like that may not occur this time, but if they do there will be no means of dealing with them. Cricket must guarantee a decision within a time that people, with other things to do, can give to them.
>
> There is a simple remedy. Why not a rule requiring a batsman to score off one of every eight consecutive

balls? The one objection that I have met to such a rule is that it would make cricket less of a solemn trial. But in these days, are we not approaching a very crisis of solemnity? **Most cricket commentators maintain an average level of solemnity far higher than most archbishops.**

Letters, JMDG. Henderson's solutions are not likely to claim the serious attention of cricketers and cricket watchers. With Einstein umpiring at the bowler's end, and batsmen skilled in mental arithmetic, his suggested "simple" rule might seem attractive. But among players more gifted in stroke-making than in mathematics, men who are playing neither French cricket nor baseball, such a suggestion must cause amusement and alarm.

An alternative suggestion is this: that in a four-day match, a maximum limit of five hours' actual play be placed on the first innings of each team. Also, I suggest that the second innings of either team be not limited, except for the ultimate time limit of the duration of the match. Quicker scoring will result, while the tactics, character, and individuality of the game would, if anything, be enhanced.

Letters, Onlooker. If the batsman fails to score off every eight balls, what then? And what about the bowler who persistently bowls off-theory?

I have often thought that it would be a good idea to have a scoring quota of so many runs per hour. This might be 60 in international games. Any deficit would be credited to the other side as penalty runs.

Also, a bowler might be required to hit the wicket or the bat with three out of every four balls bowled, any deficiency to be a penalty run to the batting side. The principle of penalty runs is not new. "No balls" present a penalty run to the batting side.

Letters, R Findlayl. In view of the enormous public interest in international cricket, the failure to protect adequately from rain an area of approximately 100 feet by eight feet seems inexplicable to a layman. After rain stopped play on Friday, the public was assured that the wicket was protected by covers, yet before noon on Saturday it was announced that parts of the wicket had been saturated, and that the bowling approaches were practically a morass.

Letters, Geo Wacey. My suggestion to brighten cricket is to paint a line down each side of the pitch to limit the width so that the ball must be within the reach of batsmen, otherwise it is counted as a wide. Then penalise the batting side one run each time a ball is not scored off. This scheme would not turn everyone into a slogger, as some seem to think, but would compel a batsman to develop strokes and the ability to pick the holes in the field. Bowlers would have to be more accurate, as a few fours would soon put the batting side well ahead and have the fielding captain searching for his most accurate bowler.

Letters, Chas Sandell. Being an enthusiast of the grand old game, I went to the Sydney Cricket Ground to see the match England versus NSW. Surely, after the lapse of ten years and all the happenings of the recent past, **a band** could have been engaged to give a fitting and well-merited welcome to a team of sportsmen who, as we know, represent a nation which saved the world.

Letters, M Rathbone. I find restful pleasure in watching cricket **as it is now played**. We get quite enough activity in our daily pursuits without wanting to watch men dashing about like disturbed ants. The scoreboard is an important feature, but I would never recognise it as the Alpha and Omega of the grand old game.

Letters, C Wickham-Laws. Hutton and Leyland at the Oval in 1938 were in complete control and scored at will, but the cricket was not thrilling. This is said, not because I am an Australian and felt glum as I watched, but because the runs were scored against an impotent attack – an attack containing two great spin bowlers in O'Reilly and Fleetwood-Smith – and impotent because of a dead, unresponsive wicket. The batting was masterly, the bowling helpless, the cricket dull.

My point is that cricket is not only batting. Lively, turning wickets will kill all the slowness of the game. Good bowlers will flourish, mediocre batsmen will fade away, class batsmen – real stroke-makers – will rise to the occasion, every run will count. The field will be on its toes, close finishes will excite, and the old game will thrive without artificial aide to life.

Letters, D Scott. Ridiculous and bizarre suggestions which your correspondents have submitted for brightening cricket are not new proposals. On reading an article written about **20 years ago** by Sir Pelham warner, I discovered the following words:

"I hope that the cricket-loving public will read and think over these suggestions before they give their approval to any radical alterations such as widening or heightening the wickets, or giving the batsman out because the bowler has been skilful enough to bowl a maiden over to him. I imagine a Test match in which Macartney had to go at the end of the first over because, forsooth, Tate had bowled a maiden over to him. To do that would be to reduce cricket to tip and run."

To the supposed cricket reformers of to-day, these words of 1926 come as a timely answer.

Apart from all this erudition, there were **some surprising events** that show up the differences between now and then.

> **Cricket news item.** Ray Lindwall, who is bowling so well, recently got exactly 100 runs in an innings. It was in a near-record time, and was the first century by a fast bowler since Jack Gregory in 1922.
>
> At the moment, Lindwall is looking for a job. He left his position of clerk in a suburban office so he could play cricket. He expects to get another job soon.
>
> Today, when the English innings had been going for half an hour, play was interrupted for ten minutes. The occasion was a visit by the Duke and Duchess of Gloucester who were able to meet the Australian team.

This is quite interesting from two points of view. **Firstly**, we have a fast bowler playing for Australia who is out of work. **Secondly**, the Royal visitors were welcomed onto the field to meet the team in the middle of a session. They certainly were more leisurely days than now.

REDS UNDER THE BEDS

Background. In 1917, a violent revolution occurred in Russia. The ruling monarchy was overthrown, and a new government of the proletariat was formed, and the Communist Party was able to introduce the actual **practice** of advanced socialism to the nation.

From the very beginning, the Western nations opposed all aspects of Communism. During WWII, however, it learned to co-exist with it, because, after some dubious moments, the Russians joined the war on the side of the Allies. When the war was over, old distrust between Russia and the West re-surfaced.

The West objected to two main matters. **Firstly**, they were worried by the fact that Russia was taking over all the small nations on its borders, and setting up Communist rule in them. **Secondly**, they were alarmed that Red political parties were being formed in every nation of the world and were, so it was claimed by the West, attempting to set up Russian-style governments therein.

As part of this process, the Australian Communist Party was small, with less support than the Greens can now muster at their very best. They only ever got one person elected to Parliament, and then only for one session.

In industry, however, they became very influential via the trade unions. In a number of industries they grabbed union leadership, and set policy for those bodies. At a time when workers wanted better conditions, and when union membership was large, the unions provided organisations that could just about match the power of the bosses. So, the Communists then started to fight with their main weapon for change. That is, **they often led their fellow Unionists out on strike**.

It is still a matter of much debate as to what the intentions of these Communists really were. There are some who say that they simply wanted better conditions and so on. The only weapon they had, they say, was the strike. On the other hand, an equal number say that they did want the strikes to cripple the state, and this would lead to a successful revolution. There is no doubt that a number of each of these types did exist.

In any case, about mid 1947, the world suddenly found that Communists were news-worthy. A year previously, they got about one or two mentions per month in major newspapers. From here on in, the number of mentions increased greatly. By June 1947, it was about 20. By December, it was 30. Even later, when Menzies and US Senator Joe McCarthy realised how much political mileage they could get out of attacking Communists, the number increased to a hundred.

In the early months, none of these attacks were at the political level. There were no diatribes against the evil plans to overthrow the Government, and thereby establish world domination. Rather, they were at the industrial level, or perhaps at the social level. The **political** attacks only came as the politicians gradually realised what a good thing they were on to.

The items below show a sample of attitudes to the embryonic anti-Communist movement. It was the beginning of the *Reds under the Beds* campaign. **The first two articles** are from the US. That nation was more advanced in its opposition to Communism, because it was more advanced in its own Capitalism. At the very beginning of the Russian revolution, in 1917, a White Army of volunteers had been formed to attempt to restore the Russian monarchy, and American citizens had supplied the bulk of the manpower and resources for that venture. Since then, the two countries had been vehemently opposed, except for the wartime intermission.

> **The US Supreme Court** today upheld the right of the Civil Service Commission to dismiss a Federal Government employee **because he is a Communist sympathiser. This employee, a Mr Freedman, had been dismissed in 1944 because there was reasonable doubt of his loyalty to the US.**

Chicago, Supreme Court Circuit. The Court today issued a ruling that stated it was libellous to describe another person or corporation a being "Communist".

The ruling stated that "the label of Communist or Communist sympathiser, in the minds of average respectable persons, places beyond the pale of respectability, and makes him a symbol of public hatred, contrary to law."

The judgement went on to say, in a six million dollar action that involved the Hearst newspapers, that **the newspapers had themselves done their utmost to create the ogre** surrounding Communism. It was hardly right for them to now say that the use of the term carried no evil connotations.

London, BBC. Early this month, the BBC agreed that the major political parties would be allowed to make some broadcasts for free in the future. It was agreed that they would be given a quota based on the number of votes they got at the last election. **The Communist Party was excluded from this agreement, on the basis that its philosophy was not consistent with British values.** Therefore today it was decided that that Party would not be allocated the one broadcast that it might otherwise be entitled to.

The Australian reaction.   With plenty of action on this front overseas, it was not likely that our local lads would miss out. Here we have an analysis from a politician.

Hobart broadcast by Premier Cosgrove. Those who are trying to spread the tenets of Communism are avowed enemies of everything worthwhile and decent in our society. The tactics of Communists and so-called militants in using their influence in the industrial movement are a challenge that the ALP cannot afford to ignore.

Direct action is now needed urgently, because the future of the Australian people is being jeopardised by the strike tactics now being employed. Pressure groups, most of which are small, have become truculent and belligerent, and by their thoughtless and unwarranted actions are rapidly slowing down the wheels of industry, causing harm to thousands of decent workers and raising the cost of living.

Now a comment from a right-wing Union leader. The State Secretary of the Australian Workers' Union said today that:

Communist agitators among the steelworkers were deliberately holding up settlement of the ICI strike at Matraville. The shortage of chemicals required for the production of dipping materials will probably result in the death of hundreds of Queensland cattle. The same position applies in NSW where there is a shortage of certain chemicals used in the drenching of sheep.

It is a national tragedy to think that because of the attitude of a few Communists, who control the steelworkers, the country is faced with grave losses, particularly in an industry which is the economic foundation of the nation.

As a fallout from a recent 30-day strike by the wharfies, a rally of workers was held in Hyde Park to express opinions. **It turned into a minor fracas**, and was handsomely labelled by the Press as a riot. The Communists were prominent among the speakers and the "thugs", and so the blame for the whole event fell on them. The incident brought forth lots of Letters to the newspapers.

Letter, E White. It would appear that there is a tremendous amount of fatuous nonsense being mouthed in the name of freedom of speech.

If we let these anarchists take over the affairs of government, we will only have ourselves to blame. They have got to be fought, and fought right now, not later; later can be too late.

If, in the name of freedom of speech, we are going to let people with a firestick roam at will throughout Australia, then we will end up with Fascism, not freedom of speech.

The *SMH* was staunchly Liberal at this stage. It said that the Domain meeting, organised by a State Liberal MP, Mr Darby, was really called to discuss how to unload masses of foodstuffs from ships that had been becalmed by the 30-day wharfies strike. The Communists had come and tried to hi-jack it. The Editorial was as violent as the strikers. It talked about "barber-gang outrages," it said that the Communists had passed from "violent propaganda to the forcible suppression of human rights", these tactics "have been employed in Europe with crushing success. Mussolini and Hitler used them with the aid of those who broke up public meetings, and bashed their opponents into insensibility." The attacks on free speech start out quite small, but they "grow in number and violence until they are in the ascendancy, until no voice can be raised against the oppressor."

The Labor Government said it was all a beat up. It was just a minor brawl, common enough at political rallies in those days. Further, that the Liberals had deliberately provoked the violence, and had been ready with the police and Press to capitalise on it. The Communists were hardly innocent by-standers, but they were very pleased to have a minor skirmish blow up into a first rate political wrangle.

The Liberal Party did its best to exploit the situation. It deplored the Communists' activities,. "Every fair-minded democratic citizen, whatever his political belief, must have been shocked at the outrageous Communist-inspired demonstration that occurred in the Domain last Tuesday. Such demonstrations only further emphasise the weakness and ineptitude of the Labor Party, which, at the expense of the community, and the housewife in particular, allows free rein to these disruptions to Australian Industry. While Labor misgoverns, there can be no peace on the waterfront or anywhere else."

In all, it was a badly orchestrated attempt to discredit the Communists.

This "riot" set the scene for the next decade. As the Communists moved more and more into politics, this scene, and the recriminations and counters, became more common. When Menzies came to power, and he realised how much political mileage he could get from slaying the Communists, the whole scenario became so overdone that it was almost comical. Menzies was able to inject more hysteria into the anti-Communist movement by talking about the international situation, with Russia gaining and abusing power in Europe, and moving southwards from South East Asia with the aim of enslaving Tasmanians.

As in America, though to a lesser extent, **no one was safe from the allegation that he was a Red**. It was hysteria, deliberately fomented at the top, that badly affected the lives of many. It was a shameful period, I think, in this nation's history. And it is a period we should all remember when Governments mount scare campaigns of any nature.

DECEMBER NEWS ITEMS

A reminder of how ugly the war had been. As the War Crimes hearings continued, it emerged that a Japanese Lieutenant at Kavieng in New Ireland received orders that **he should execute 17 Australian prisoners.** He had no swords, and rifle shots would have disclosed their position to Allied forces. So he issued instructions that **the men be killed by Jiu jitsu and strangulation**. The orders were carried out, though **the process involved two hours of suffering. Lest We Forget.**

In NSW, local council elections were held throughout the State. There was one really big surprise. The Prime Minister, Chifley, had also held **a council seat in Abercrombie Shire since 1932. But he was defeated for that seat at the council elections**, by an Independent. Was this **a sign of things to come** when his Party would go to the national polls? Liberal pundits were happily saying "yes".

A Melbourne man was seated on a tram when a bump jostled a standing passenger onto the man's lap. But the standing passenger was eating fish and chips out of a newspaper, and **a bone in the fish pierced the finger of the passenger. He was carted off to hospital, where the bone was removed** under a local anaesthetic.

United States negro servicemen serving in Britain **left behind 10,000 coloured children** when they returned to the US. These children were having great difficulties in living in Britain. **5,000 of them will be shipped to the US on a liner soon,** and will be **"fostered out"**to their fathers and the general population. This deal was arranged by the so-called Anti-slavery Society.

Doctor Herbert Evatt, fresh from his stint at the United Nations, arrived back in Australia. **He was questioned about the UN's future**, given that it had so far achieved no peace in trouble-spots such as India, Palestine, Indonesia and Paris. It was only two year old. Did it have a future? Or would it go the same way as the League of Nations had gone?....

The idealistic Evatt had no worry at all. **"No doubt about it", he said.** It turned out that he was right, though its path has not always been easy. The saving question was always **"What could replace it?"**

At Sydney's Rookwood Cemetery, **80 grave diggers** today completed the grisly task of **disintering 1,000 bodies of American Servicemen, and sending them back to the United States....**

At the end of a fortnight's work, they were paid out. But **four armed thieves** forced their way into the cemetery's office, and demanded the entire payroll. Sorry, old chap, but the money has already been paid out. All they got was **the wages paid to the three men in the office.**

Christmas pantomimes were back. They had gone away during the war, but all the big cities now had a few to choose from. **Pretty girls dressed as men. Burly men in their skirts and blouses.** It's a wonder there wasn't a law against it. Today, there might be.

PALESTINE

Prior to World war II, a map of the world shows patches of pink spread liberally round the four corners of the globe. The British Empire was everywhere. In some cases – like Australia, Canada, New Zealand, and for the whites in South Africa – it was welcome. In others, indeed in most cases, it was at best tolerated, because of the military might and the political dominance that it brought with it. During the war, many of these dissatisfied countries supported Britain on condition (express or implied) that some form of self-government or independence would be granted when victory came. Now, in 1947, some of these countries started to agitate for a rapid turn-over of power.

The Brits were generally quite sensible about this. Some of the more extreme, of course, wanted to maintain all the grandeur and power of former years. These were well in the minority. Also in the minority were those who wanted to simply pull out of some places without heed for the consequences. The policy adopted was to prepare – in the haphazard way that humans always manage – for independence, and when the circumstances seemed right enough, to hand over power. But Britons were becoming conscious that the cost of maintaining an unwilling Empire was now beyond their means, and that lingering longer than necessary was not an option.

In Palestine, the British had held a mandate over the country since 1917. At that time, it had endorsed the so-called Balfour Declaration that virtually guaranteed that Jews would have rights to a Jewish National Home in the area of Palestine. By the end of World War II, this promise from the British had become a demand from Jews worldwide for an independent state, centred round their traditional home of Jerusalem. The number of Jews in Palestine at that time was only half that of the Arab population, though there was great and violent agitation for that nation – still under the control of the British – to allow entry to hundreds of thousands of Jewish settlers who had been uprooted by Hitler. **They wanted this new state for security against any future Hitlers.**

By 1947, the British announced that they would get out of this mess in May, 1948, and they passed the matter over to the youthful United Nations. This body had only been established in early 1946, and **was still wet behind the ears**. It set up a Committee that recommended a most complex plan to divide Palestine into three Arab areas, and three Jewish areas. This scheme was abhorrent to all concerned, so it was pigeon-holed, and the UN was out of any real involvement for two decades.

Throughout 1947 and 1948, the Jews gradually took control of Palestine and Jerusalem by force. In this they were materially assisted by the support of the US, which had millions of American Jews watching with interest as the situation unfolded. By the end of 1948, Israel had fully conquered, by armed force, the Palestinian areas, forcing mass evacuations of Palestinians from the new State of Israel.

The conquest of the Arabs **so easily** surprised the world. Of course, no one expected the one million Arabs living in Palestine to put up much resistance, because they were so few in numbers, and they had no effective weapons.

But the Arab nations all round them came to their rescue. There was Egypt, Lebanon, Syria, Iraq, Transjordan, and Iran. All of these, some to a lesser extent, got involved and sent off their armies to preserve Arab hegemony. But they failed, and in fact were humiliated. Their trouble was that they all went in with their own self-interest to the fore. For example, Transjordan came out of it with control over extra territory, and, incidentally, took the opportunity to call its enlarged kingdom by its modern name of Jordan. None of these nations made a serious attempt to unify the various forces, and as a result, simply lost the First Arab Israeli war with consummate ease.

This Chapter does not focus on that part of the story. It goes back to the period of late 1946, and 1947, when the Israelis were intent on getting rid of the British. The incidents I report are part of a series that grew progressively worse until the British started to withdraw in 1947, and fully withdrew in 1948, when the modern state of Israel was proclaimed. It is interesting to note that the English-speaking Press referred to these activities of protest as **terrorist** acts, and at the time, **the Jews**, who could also be called freedom-fighters, were nominated as the **terrorists**.

Labour Party Conference, Bournemouth, England. The Foreign Secretary, Mr Bevin, told the Labour Party Conference that he was **not** prepared to allow the entry of another 100,000 Jewish persons into Palestine, as was strongly supported by the United States. He stated that if he did so, he would be required to put another division of troops there, and he could see no corresponding benefits from this.

I am extremely grateful to the US for taking part in the Palestine Commission. The agitation there, particularly in New York – and I do not want the Americans to misunderstand me – is because **they do not want too many of them in New York**.

The financial issues involved in the Palestine business are huge. The British Chancellor of the Exchequor cannot carry the burden. We cannot take on another 200,000 Pound expenditure in Palestine, that is what is really involved.

News item, Jerusalem. The kidnapping of five British officers from The Officers' Club in Tel Aviv is a plain indication that the well-trained, well-equipped, and well-disciplined Jewish terrorist army is now in action. These terrorists are chiefly drawn from Palmath, the inner-ring "shock-troop" organisation of Haganah, the Jewish illegal army. Their object is to make Palestine a Jewish state, and they believe this can be done by wearing down the British administration by terrorism.

The kidnapped officers are certainly being held as hostages, and it is likely they will be executed if the British confirm the death sentence passed last week on two Jewish terrorists.

British Military, London. British authorities arrested two thousand Jewish persons in a number of raids today, aimed at avoiding anarchy that threatened under a siege from terrorists. The British High Commissioner in Palestine, announced in a broadcast, a solemn warning that Britain was resolved to root out terrorism and violence in Palestine.

Palestine Police, Jerusalem. Eighty eight persons have been killed when two bombs exploded in the cellars of the King David Hotel in Jerusalem today, according to a Palestinian Police communiqué. Five floors were completely destroyed. The Hotel is the site of the British Military Headquarters in Palestine. Dozens of civilians, and scores of military personnel were also injured by the blast, and now hundreds of troops are working frantically in the search for more bodies that are certain to be found in the wreckage.

News item, Jerusalem. Only a few hours before the London Conference on Palestine was due to begin, wailing sirens woke Jerusalem from uneasy slumbers this morning to announce that terrorists and saboteurs were again at work.

In a widespread series of carefully co-ordinated explosions, these terrorists temporarily paralysed rail traffic throughout Palestine. The secret radio of Irgun Zvai Leumi, largest Jewish terrorist group, claimed responsibility, and said "This is the end of the truce." The line was cut in 20 or 30 places.

News item, Haifa. Another inhumanly-crowded "hell ship" attempting to bring in illegal Jewish immigrants into Palestine was emptied of its cargo yesterday, and lies under arrest in Haifa Harbour alongside a dozen other craft.

The small 400-ton caique, so rotten that it could almost be torn apart with the hands, was crammed with 1,200 Jews, many times the number such a ship should carry. All were suffering from thirst because fresh water ran out three days off Palestine. Several men who had drunk sea water were raving deliriously.

House of Commons, London. The number of Jews gathering **in the United States zone in Germany and Austria** in preparation for a journey to Palestine almost amounts to a second Exodus, says a report from a group of Members of the House of Commons. The report says there is a highly organised group of Jews in Austria whose presence endangers public order. The report goes on to say that this movement to

Palestine is well funded from American sources, and has a great deal of influence behind it.

Mixed Editorials. The flogging by Jewish desperadoes of British soldiers, one of them a field officer twice decorated for gallantry, calls for an immediate tightening of British control in Palestine. These outrages are not isolated incidents – they are part of a policy of provocation and terrorism which has in the past involved the murder of Lord Mayne, the attempted assassination of the High Commissioner, and the deaths of many British soldiers and police.

Such a sharp blow to Britain's prestige, particularly among Eastern peoples, must be countered by swift and drastic action. The insult to the King's uniform is not to be tolerated, and besides, these and kindred terrorist activities constitute a flagrant defiance of the peace and order which Britain, however unwillingly, has accepted the responsibility of maintaining.

This situation continued on and on, and persisted long after the British had started to leave. Then the attention of the "freedom fighters" turned to the Palestinian population who still remained in Jewish lands, and was no less violent.

Back in Australia, most Jews were keen not to be associated with the violence.

Letters, Neo Josephus Flavious. The identification of the Jews in Australia with Zionism is misleading. It is true that the Zionists are, as everywhere, the most vociferous and practically the only organised group among the Jews in Australia.

But there remains this hard fact: among the 35,000 persons of the Jewish faith living in Australia, only 7,500 found it worth while to make even the gesture of paying the "shekel" of two shillings a year for their allegiance to the Zionist cause.

More than that, when the Zionists recently held elections for their World Congress at Basle, despite all the agitation, only 2,000 Jews in the whole of Australia voted. Nevertheless, three delegates, elected by only seven per cent of Australian Jews, went to Basle to represent supposedly all the Jews here.

No Rabbinical pathos can change these figures, nor can it miss the correct interpretation, which is that the **vast majority of people of the Jewish faith here no not wish to mix their old religious tradition with radical chauvinistic nationalism**, showing clearly all the characteristics of religious decay and moral degeneration.

Loyal Australians of the Jewish faith, knowing no other loyalty at heart but that for the country they are living in and working for, should not be robbed of the precious sympathy of Australian democrats and Christians because of the self-destructive misdeeds of criminals in Palestine.

This theme was popular in Australia. Many Jews here, and I think it was the great majority of them, were anxious to say that they did not associate themselves with the violence that was widespread in Palestine. They wanted their credentials as true-blue Aussies to be recognised here, while at the same time maintaining their religious ties with the Jews in Palestine.

Letters, S Price. The reports of the crimes committed by the terrorist groups in Palestine must stir the hearts and minds of every British subject with disgust and indignation. Quite undoubtedly, among the most indignant must be numbered, with very few exceptions, the members of the Jewish faith. As a representative member of that faith, I would like to express the views of myself and the great number of my co-religionists, who have requested me to do so.

In every political and spiritual creed there is, and always will be, a minority which, though small, is sufficient to contaminate the majority, however great. To the very great majority of Jews – in fact, to almost all who have lived, perhaps for generations, under English rule – England is their mother country. As has been proved in the two great world wars of this century, British Jews have flocked enthusiastically to the support of England. Unfortunately loyalty, as are most of the decencies of life, is silent, whereas the raucous voice of one renegade can be shouted from the rooftops.

It is to be hoped that the citizens of this country recognise that the Australian Jew **is** an Australian, and that his faith is something that he confines entirely to his spiritual world. Australia is his country, and Judaism is his faith. Spiritually he is as the members of any other faith or religion.

So our Australian Jews testified to their innocence of the violence. Of course, they wanted to see the independent State established, but they wanted this to be done without looking down the barrels of rifles.

Over the years, as the battles between the Israelis and Palestinians have gone on and on, they have, to their credit, maintained that attitude. Let us all hope that one day soon this troubled part of the world will find the peace that everyone there wants so desperately.

SUMMING UP 1947

Babies starting to boom. Right from the early 1930's, the population of Australia was growing at a steady rate. For example, from 1940 to 1941, it grew by 70,000 a year, and from 1941 to 1946 it also grew by 70,000 a year. But the war ended, and the service-people came home and got on with their business, and so the number of births rocketed. In 1947, there was a population increase of 120,000. By 1951, the annual increase had risen to 240,000. It stayed that high, or higher, for the next fifteen years. Granted, in the later years, some of it was from net migration, but pre-1950 the increase was primarily due to what I will call natural forces.

So, here we are at the beginning of the Baby Boom. If anyone was smart enough to anticipate the boom happening, then they would be smart enough to work out that the influx of so many new mouths to feed would be a stimulus to the economy, and that growth would happen. But none of these sages foresaw the other changes that came one after another over the years.

Let me give a few examples. **Looking back**, we can see the diminishing respect for authority, as exemplified by the cutting of the ties to the British Empire and the Crown. And the changes to religious attitudes that saw church attendances drop, and the rampant secularism of today develop. **Looking back**, we can see how the population welcomed greater opportunities for education, and the old rigidities there were swept aside. **Looking back**, we can see the development of the women's movement, and the transformation of family life as more women took up positions in the workforce. **Looking back**, we can see how the contraceptive pill changed the love life of women and men alike, and how "modern" medicine, and all sorts of machines and inventions lengthened our lives. And, to cut this list short, we can see how the Beatles, and the hula hoop, and ten-pin bowling lightened-up our lives.

None of this small sample of changes was apparent at the end of 1947. Up until the war, the world had been the same, more or less, for decades. All the old institutions seemed very secure, the same old newspapers were all the time preaching to the conservatives, the Churches still thundered away at the sinners, among a population that had no inkling of what sin really was. Catholics still would go to hell if they ate meat on Friday. Unofficial censorship was endemic; more people committed rape than talked about it, more people had sex than talked about it.

In this litany of repression, let me single out one group. At the end of the war, there was a lot of talk about new beginnings, about how we could come out from this valley of tears, about great opportunities. To do this in a political sense would be against the odds, but if ever there was a time to do so, this would be it. Surely, even working within our old institutions, we could put aside party differences, and come up with some grand policies for a new future, some attempt to ameliorate the lot of the vastly under-privileged, some vision that would unite the nation. But these politicians of ours gave no inkling of this.

The Labor Party, with its smoke-filled back-rooms, had their Caucuses filled with Arthur Calwells, who wanted to deport the now famous Mrs O'Keefe, who was married to an Australian, and had borne eight children by him. The Liberals wanted, as their Holy Grail, to ban Communists and save Tasmania from Stalin. The State politicians set up police forces that had some of their best policemen waiting round in public lavatories at night trying to entrap poofters.

The politicians simply went back to their old ways, and right now, in 2020, they have not got one bit better. This, on reflection, is not so much a criticism of the individuals. After all, they were not evil people nor were they stupid people, and generally they mean well. It is **the system** that we were locked into, and would be very difficult to break. Let me add that, sadly, this is even more true at international level. It was too much to hope, even in those somewhat heady days of 1947, that major political institutions might change. I suppose in reality that they are simply here to stay.

But after all this, let me point out that 1947, to me, was the start of a renaissance. This had its inception in the war years. For example, among the men, they had lost much respect for the British officers who directed them and led them into disasters such as Greece and Singapore. They stood firmly behind Curtin when he wanted, over Churchill's resistance, to bring our troops back home. What I am saying is that such incidents lessened their automatic acceptance of authority. The same for women. When they were called to duty, they learned that they **could** do men's jobs, that they could live away from home, they could make their own money.

These are all little instances, but put them all together and they make up the changes to authority, and to religion, and to the womens' movement, and to family life that I talked about earlier. It was in 1947 that people started to think, actually think, about these matters. In that year, you got the first few Letters talking about our position relative to Britain, and a big increase in the percentage of Letters criticising the Churches.

People were forgetting the war, and now were turning to begetting babies, to looking after babies, and saving for a mortgage, and building a new house. Life was becoming exciting, and each and every person was doing it for themselves. Society had suddenly got more mobile, it was possible to change jobs, and if you crawled hard and long to a bank manager, you could get a loan. It was becoming a new world, one that offered the prospect for young parents to live much more exciting lives than their parents, and achieve a measure of wealth undreamt of by their parents. Besides, there were now, or soon, washing machines, and refrigerators that worked, and, for the men, electric lawn mowers and then petrol-driven ones. And they could throw away the old crank handle when they got that new car. What a world to live in.

So 1947 closed with perhaps an inkling that big things were ahead. But no one knew the truth and extent of the revolutions in attitudes and ideas that were to follow. If they had, if they had foreseen the world now, with all its warts, **would they have wanted to get off?** You, the reader, will have your own opinion, but my bet is that they would not have got off for any money.

In 1953, pets in churches were welcomed with open arms. Painless childbirth was popular, especially among women. Be warned - the coronation of Elizabeth will soon be in the news. Edmund Hillary reached the top. Thallium became popular, as a footballer found out. Lots of Pom migrants had done their time, and went back to Mother England.

In 1954, Queen Elizabeth II was sent here

victorious, and Petrov was our very own spy - what a thrill. Boys were being sentenced to life. Johnny Ray cried all the way to the bank. Church halls were being used for dirty dancing. Open the pubs after six? Were they ever shut? A-bombs had scaredies scared.

****

Chrissi and birthday books for Mum and Dad and Aunt and Uncle and cousins and family and friends and work and everyone else.

Don't forget a good read and chuckle for yourself.

At boombooks.biz

In 1955, be careful of the demon drink, get your brand new Salk injections, submit your design for the Sydney Opera house now, prime your gelignite for another Redex Trial, and stop your greyhounds killing cats. Princess Margaret shocked the Church, Huxley shocked the Bishops, and our Sundays are far from shocking.

****

AVAILABLE AT ALL GOOD BOOK STORES AND NEWS AGENTS